HOME ON THE RANGE

Memories of Okaton, South Dakota

JAMES E ROGHAIR

iUniverse®

HOME ON THE RANGE
MEMORIES OF OKATON, SOUTH DAKOTA

iUniverse books may be ordered through booksellers or by contacting:

iUniverse
1663 Liberty Drive
Bloomington, IN 47403
www.iuniverse.com
844-349-9409

ISBN: 978-1-6632-5502-0 (sc)
ISBN: 978-1-6632-5504-4 (hc)
ISBN: 978-1-6632-5503-7 (e)

Library of Congress Control Number: 2023913688

Print information available on the last page.

iUniverse rev. date: 09/08/2023

Contents

Appendix

Introduction

Home on the Range: Memories of Okaton, South Dakota

This book is a collection of memories of my first fourteen years (1943-1957) growing up on a wheat farm near Okaton, South Dakota, in the western part of Jones County. These stories are a glimpse into life in our home and community.

My earliest childhood memory is my second birthday in January 1945 while I was staying in my grandparents' home. I was encircled by a crowd of tall aunties in front of Grandma Roghair's coal-burning kitchen range; there were Aunts Joanna, Janetta, Alice, and Gertrude. Aunt Harriet was working as a nurse, perhaps in Bismark, North Dakota, and Aunt Hilda was probably in Denver working for Northwest Orient Airlines.

One of the aunts in the circle gave me an envelope from my mother. She was seventy-five miles away, boarding in a private home near the hospital in Pierre and awaiting the birth of her second baby, my brother Gene. I had little or no experience receiving or opening mail addressed to me, so one aunt helped me. Inside was a birthday card from my mother. Receiving it was especially dramatic for me with so many young women watching and coaching me. That moment is etched unforgettably in my mind, and I still have the card to verify the memory.

Although I was excited by the card, I didn't understand why my mother was not present. At that age, I had no idea how my life would change when I saw her again. Gene Henry Roghair was born about two weeks after my birthday, and after another two weeks or so, he and Mom were released from the hospital. I do not have a memory of Dad's bringing Mom and Gene back from Pierre and picking me up to return home together.

I was surely happy to be reunited with my parents. But I had spent about a month living in Grandpa and Grandma's home, being the center of attention for my grandparents, four aunts, and my three youngest uncles—Bob, Ted, and Bill. Coming home to share my parents' attention with a new brother was a little more than I was ready for. Jealous, as any two-year-old might be, I managed to get myself up to the bassinet in the living room where Gene lay, and I bit him on the cheek. I had surely been instructed to give him a kiss. Mom scolded me, and I scrambled down. (I don't think I ever bit Gene again.)

These are my two earliest memories, the birthday card and biting Gene. My third memory blurs with the second, because it was also set in our living room. Mom was sitting beside Gene in the bassinet, and I stood nearby. I remember our breathless anticipation. Dad standing tall at a full six-foot two, proudly pulled the chain of a living room electric fixture he had installed. The bulb came on; we had light! Before, it had only been kerosene lamps. Now we had bare ceiling bulbs, not only in the living room, but over the kitchen table and range, in the front hall, and in the two bedrooms.

Dad had purchased a Wincharger and mounted it on a wooden tower a little taller than the house. It was a generator with two blades, shaped much like the propeller of a small airplane, and directed into the wind by a broad steel tail. The six-volt direct current it produced was transmitted into the house through two thick, heavily insulated wires, one positive and the other negative. The "juice," was stored in three two-volt wet-cell batteries in the cellar. It was not the 110-volt power they had in the towns, but it was a start. I can't remember seeing Dad doing the installation before this breakthrough moment, but this would be only one of many improvements he would make in the coming years.

We lived on prairieland, only a few miles north of the White River, although we were in the watershed of the Bad River several miles to the north. We were about midway between the Missouri River and the Badlands National Monument. Both the 1940s and 1950s versions of

US Highway 16 and their later replacement, Interstate 90, bordered or passed through our family's farmland. This major transcontinental route between Chicago and Seattle crossed the state about one quarter of the way north of South Dakota's southern border.

I share these stories from my childhood, true as I remember them, with a sense of place and my life in it. During the intervening decades much has changed in me and in the way the people still living in my home community live, and yet much remains the same. The rolling hills and the long views persist, as does the determination of those who live on its special landscape. I hope to capture for you a sense of how I experienced my early years over half a century ago.

Our small home was located on an 800-acre farm—five times the size of the early twentieth-century homesteads, but minuscule compared to twenty-first century farms. The cash crop was winter wheat. We had animals, too—a few beef cattle, a milk cow, a horse, a dog, and cats. We usually had small flocks of chickens and ducks. Occasionally we had a few pigs or sheep. A vegetable garden, hay fields, pastureland, and assorted other crops rounded out our typical family farm. There was no running water, indoor plumbing, commercial electricity or telephone. But we did not feel deprived; we had everything that we needed. Life for us was complete and as it should be living on the prairie.

As a child growing up, I felt I was part of this land, and it was a part of me. Like many children, my loyalties were to our home on the small family farm, to our Okaton community, and to South Dakota. I could not imagine living anywhere else or having any other life. I expected to become a farmer like my dad. I even imagined that I would inherit some of the community and church responsibilities that I watched my father and grandfather fulfill. I didn't begin to wrestle with any competing life choices until my early teen years.

Our community's history had been brief. Most of the original homesteaders arrived in 1906, only thirty-seven years before I was born. The Milwaukee Railroad spur line between Huron, South Dakota, and the Black Hills had opened the territory to settlers. A few had arrived a little earlier by covered wagon, some of whom helped build the railroad. The county's weekly newspaper, *The Murdo Coyote*, which is still published, claims its origin in 1904.

As we grew up, we children heard a few stories about the first settlers, and even knew some of them. But my family's history in the region had been even briefer. My paternal grandparents and their growing family arrived in 1925, when they purchased a previously homesteaded 160-acre farm with its small house.

Anything dated before my parents were born seemed to be ancient history to me as a child. So, in the summer of 1956, I wasn't duly impressed by how relatively short the fifty-year history of our county was. But my immediate family proudly participated in the celebrations of the founding of the county's two largest towns. My brother Gene and I were part of an eight-person square dance group performing on the main street of Murdo, the Jones County seat. Later, a few miles east, on an outdoor stage in the town of Draper, I played the Hawaiian guitar and sang a popular tune with my siblings Gene, Crystal, and Wallace. Our own town of Okaton had also been settled in 1906 but had no celebration of its own, since by 1956 it had dwindled to about sixty people. Its residents and the nearby farmers and ranchers went to events in the larger towns. (As I write this memoir, the townsite of Okaton now has only a few residents. According to the 2020 Census, Okaton is now in a thirty-square mile tract with thirty-one residents.)

Of course, from an adult perspective, it is easy to recognize how short the histories of our communities were—and still are. But now, as I reflect on our 1956 celebrations, I realize that as we commemorated the communities' histories, there was not even a nod to the previous residents. Native American people and their cultures had thrived on this land for generations—perhaps millennia—before European immigrants arrived.

The night I left South Dakota at the age of fourteen, I shed a tear. How could I become a part of any other state? I feared I would never return to my childhood environment, and my sense of oneness with my surroundings was being shattered. Nevertheless, life continued, and it has been rich.

The Structure of This Book

As I share these stories with my readers, I want to share with you how we lived, what we did, and what was important to us. With the encouragement and critique of two writing groups, I have been writing, rewriting, and editing these stories for several years. Written separately, they have been brought together as chapters of this collection. The stories are arranged by major themes, rather than in strict chronological order.

Because of this structure, it is not necessary to follow a plot line from beginning to end. Each story can stand alone. Although details may at times overlap, I have tried not to repeat unnecessarily, but to provide a smooth read. As I share this book of memories with audiences beyond my family and home community, I offer the timeline below. It provides major points of reference to give the reader a perspective on the chronology of events in the stories I tell—and the world I grew up in.

"Home on the Range"

When I was a boy "Home on the Range" was a hit song:

> Oh, give me a home where the buffalo roam,
>   Where the deer and the antelope play,
> Where seldom is heard a discouraging word,
>   And the skies are not cloudy all day.
> Home, home on the range . . .

"In 1933 President Franklin D. Roosevelt claimed it to be his favorite song. Since then [it] has been sung by everyone from Willie Nelson to Porky Pig," according to the Kansas State Historical Society website. It confirms that "Home on the Range" was adopted as the Kansas State Song in 1947. The poem by Brewster M. Higley, first published in 1874 and later set to music by his friend Daniel E. Kelley, was said to be inspired by Higley's experience on his own Kansas homestead—likely not so different from those in our part of South Dakota.

So, on the broad, windswept prairies of Jones County, South Dakota, in the 1940s and '50s, our community joined everyone else in the country to claim that song as our own. We, too, loved our home on the range. The song was a part of 4-H Club meetings, school classes and other social gatherings. I assumed its words were about our time and place. It did not occur to me that they expressed more nostalgia than reality in our experience.

There were certainly no herds of roaming buffalo or playing deer and antelope. I remember seeing a single deer beside a dirt road near our home. It hung around for a few weeks and was such an unusual sight that neighbors stopped their cars to observe it—or to even try to feed it. Any buffalo still living were more than 100 miles from our home, and the nearest antelope, maybe even farther. Our land was farm ground and cow pasture.

As I share these stories of our life on the range, I invite you, the reader, into the world of my family and our neighbors. Together we indeed enjoyed living where seldom was heard a discouraging word and the skies were not cloudy all day.

Welcome to our world,
James E Roghair

Chronological References
for
Home on the Range: Memories of Okaton, South Dakota

October 1912

– Edward Roghair (Ed, Dad) born, Sibley, IA.

October 1916

– Margaret Bowder (Peggy, Mom) born, Timber Lake, SD.

Spring 1925

– Henry and Cornelia Roghair (my grandparents) move from northwest Iowa to Okaton, SD with their family.

May 1927

– Dad graduates 8th grade, Okaton, SD, and starts to farm. (In the next few years, he takes two winter courses on diesel mechanics in Fargo, ND.)

May 1934

– Mom graduates High School, Timber Lake, SD.

May 1940

– Mom receives a 2-year teaching certificate from Northern State Teachers College, Aberdeen, SD. (Her first year of higher education was at the SD State College at Brookings. She had spent some time working in a doctor's office in Timber Lake before college.)

September 1940

– Mom begins teaching the primary room of Okaton School and meets my dad.

June 1941

- My parents marry in Timber Lake, returning to live in the Okaton area—first in the school teacherage, then briefly on the Lobdell place.

Spring 1942

- My parents move to their own farm 3½ miles northwest of Okaton.

January 1943

- Son James (Jim, me) born in the hospital in Chamberlain, SD.

February 1945

- Son Gene (my brother) born in the hospital in Pierre, SD. I stay with Roghair grandparents at the time of his birth.

July 1947

- Daughter Crystal (Crysti, my sister) born in the hospital in Pierre, SD; Grandma Crystal Bowder stays with us at time of her birth.

September 1949

- I start first grade in Okaton School (then 12 grades).

Spring 1950

- Reconstruction of US 16 begins.

September 1951

- Gene begins first grade in Okaton School (now 8 grades and one teacher, upgraded to two teachers by Thanksgiving because of influx of students from families of road construction crew).

January 1952

- Historic Blizzard of 1952.

May 1952

- Massive Flooding on Missouri River.
- Son Wallace (Wally, my brother) born in hospital in Pierre; Bowder grandparents, Frank and Crystal, stay with us at time of his birth.

Spring 1952

- Rural Electric Association (REA), electrical power arrives in the area.

Summer 1952

- I take swimming lessons in Aberdeen, SD.

September 1953

- Crysti begins first grade, Okaton School, (now 1 teacher with all elementary grades).

October 1953

- Prairie Ranchers 4-H Club organized.

Spring 1955

- I begin driving the tractor doing summer fallow work.

May 1957

- Family trip to Oregon, and decision to move.

September 1957

- I take train to Oregon to start high school.

October 1957

- Family moves to McMinnville, OR.

Thanks and Credits

I thank the following publications for permission to re-print chapters that have been previously published. (Some are slightly edited.)

- Chapter 1 was published in *Two-Cylinder Magazine*, Jan–Feb 2013, and is used with permission.
- The following chapters appeared in *The Murdo Coyote*: Chapter 9, Aug 1, 2019; Chapter 15, Oct 20, 2016; Chapter 28 ran serially Jan 12, 19, and 26, 2017. All used with permission.
- Chapter 14 appeared as a winning story in "Pasatiempo" of the *Santa Fe New Mexican*, Dec 27, 2012-Jan 2, 2013, and used with permission.
- Chapter 39 was a Jones County eighth grade graduation assignment for the author.
- Chapter 40 was written but never published by the author's brother Gene H. Roghair and is used with permission.
- Chapter 41 was written by author's late mother under her name Margaret Roghair and published in *South Dakota Magazine*, Jul/Aug,2010 and used with permission.
- Chapter 42 was written by the author's sister, Crystal Shoji and appeared in *Dakota Roghairs* by Dee LeRoye, Dakota Rose Publishing, 2006. I have received editor's permission to use anything from that book and permission from my sister for this poem.

I thank two groups of writers who have helped me refine these stories. The first grew out of a Memoir Writing course at Renesan in Santa Fe, NM. The group began with about a dozen writers, but three of us continued for several years: Ursala Moeller, the late Frances Hunter, and I.

After that group dissolved, I was invited by the late Margaret Walsh to join another writing group. After Margaret's death, I have continued to work with Colin Barker and Bruce Moss as I have completed the book manuscript.

I, also, thank various individuals for assisting me in many ways:

My wife, Elizabeth Byers Roghair, has assisted with editing the manuscript.

To verify my memories, I have checked some facts with my three siblings, Gene and Wallace Roghair and Crystal Roghair Shoji, my late cousin Melvin Roghair and his wife Clarice Caldwell Roghair (Dee LeRoye), my cousins Cornelia Roghair, Richard Roghair, and Charlotte Bowder Rose, and fellow students at Okaton School, Lucy Crazy Bear Slycord, Douglas Tedrow, and Wayne Arp.

Information written by various Roghair family members found in *Dakota Roghairs* edited by Dee LeRoy (Clarise Roghair) and a few notes written by my parents have been helpful.

The Jones County History Facebook page and its followers, and *Okaton School Bulldog* annuals have been helpful.

Many internet sources have been consulted, to affirm and clarify facts. I mention some of them: several *Wikipedia* articles, the Kansas State Historical Society website, an online obituary of B.D. Dykstra, Ancestry. com, Classic Sewing Magazine, 2016.

PART A

Prologue to Adventure

ONE

John Deere Day

John Deere Day was a yearly highlight for my brother Gene and me. In the mid-1950s, we always got out of school to accompany Dad to the event in the movie theater in Murdo, the county seat. Ordinarily the theater was only open for movies on Saturday nights. That's when farm families and their employees, if any, would come. Almost everyone came to town on Saturday nights. Not only was the theater open, but so were the stores, and, of course, the pool hall. But on John Deere Day, the theater was open for a special mid-day, mid-week event.

Each year, we saw the latest John Deere Day Movie, a tradition that went back to 1930 and continued into the 1960s. The annual films were a great marketing tool to promote the company's newest agricultural machines. The John Deere Day tradition was a strong pillar supporting staunch brand loyalty. Many families like ours were *John Deere-only*.

Attendees saw machines they could use on their own farms but also glimpsed machines unheard of in their locale. I particularly remember seeing cotton pickers—quite a novelty and unrelated to anything in our South Dakota dry-land wheat farming. Going to John Deere Day was like taking a trip to unknown and exotic lands. Dad, although having only completed the eighth grade, had developed an insatiable curiosity about almost any subject. I know he considered the annual John Deere excursion an educational opportunity for his children and so, without qualms, he took us out of school to attend.

I can't remember my mother ever coming to John Deere Day. We didn't question that. It didn't seem like anything she would be interested in, and I don't remember any other women being there. After all, farming was Dad's thing—not hers. It was always Dad, and never Mom, who operated the tractor, who made decisions about what to plant and how to till the land. John Deere Day seemed a natural male experience—a guys' day out.

One custom in our John Deere Day experiences solidified its male orientation. Although Mom never let us have coffee, the only refreshments offered in the lobby of the theater on those days were coffee and doughnuts. So when Gene and I attended, totally supervised by Dad, we each had doughnuts and a cup of coffee with lots of cream and sugar. Never mind that it was common knowledge in our family and community that coffee wasn't good for kids: "It will stunt your growth. It will make your stomach turn black." But that was all suspended for John Deere Day.

It is with fondness that I remember those experiences shared with Dad. However, it never occurred to me to think about Dad's experiences before I was born. But in 1991, when Mom and Dad were celebrating their fiftieth wedding anniversary, Uncle Bob, Dad's youngest brother—closer in age to me than he was to Dad—wrote information, news to me, in my parent's anniversary book. Speaking of my dad, Bob remembered, "Ed bought his new model 'A' John Deere tractor in the late '30s. He'll have to give the exact year as I was quite small. But I remember being very proud of the new tractor, and looking back I think he was, too. I didn't think it amounted to much with those skinny skeleton wheels on it," referring to the cogged steel wheels, standard before rubber tires became standard. "The Roghair clan has been buying John Deere ever since."

2

Dad, the oldest son, had started a family tradition of loyalty which his father adopted, as have at least three more generations of the family still farming. John Deere Day annually fostered that loyalty.

Bob made a surprising addition to his story. Just a few years after Dad had purchased his first tractor, "The whole primary room had the treat of going to John Deere Day with Ed as chauffer when Miss Bowder [Mom] was teaching." My youngest uncles Bob and Ted were in the second and third grade in the classroom of Miss Bowder in the Okaton, South Dakota, School in 1940-41. It was the only year she taught before she married Dad and became a farm wife. Bob added, "In later years, I never could figure out what John Deere Day had to do with school, but we sure didn't complain at the time."

Remembering my 1950s experience of John Deere Day as a guys' day out, I never would have imagined it as part of my parents' courtship! They must have made quite a spectacle in the small crowd of men who all knew each other. Uncle Bob tactfully remembered, "Farm wives usually stayed home and had a day to themselves."

I can only imagine the ribbing Dad got for bringing the young teacher and her students. Likely our Uncle Albert, another of Dad's brothers, who would later go off to the Army in World War II, led the joking, "Ed, was that the school *marm* sitting so close to you in the John Deere movie? Is she going to drive your tractor this year?" And knowing Albert, he found occasion to rib Mom, too. No one was exempt from Albert's humor.

Ribbing or no, Ed and Margaret Roghair's experiences of John Deere Day set the stage for their sixteen years of South Dakota farming together. It foreshadowed their shared involvement, toward the end of their sixty-five-year marriage, in working toward the new Yamhill County Historical Museum in McMinnville, Oregon. It has a growing display of farm tractors, a significant number of which are John Deeres. Neither Mom nor Dad lived to see the new museum completed, but it is a rich

3

legacy of their life together, and a breakroom for staff and volunteers has been named in their honor.

As I reflect on their 1940s experience, I wonder whether things are so different when young people are in love that even John Deere Day with a bunch of little kids could be a part of courtship. Or was it that Dad, at the age of twenty-eight, was so enamored of the educational value of John Deere Day that he spontaneously offered to take his two brothers and the other pupils in the primary class? If so, taking their teacher just went with his project. It is too late to ask Mom or Dad for their recollections, so the truth of the matter will remain a mystery, and we can each draw our own conclusions.

I wonder, did the primary class all get coffee that day?

Brothers Bill, Ed, and Albert Roghair and their
John Deeres about 1940.

Brothers Bob and Ted Roghair on two other John Deeres in the 1950s.

Margaret Bowder (Mom) and the primary class. Boys
in overalls are my uncles Ted and Bob Roghair. One
girl was absent when picture was taken.

TWO

My Great-Grandpa John Henry Addison Swearingen

"Grandpa Swearingen came to visit when we were newlyweds," Mom told me shortly before she died. They were living in half the teacherage, which had been Okaton's original school building. Mom said, "It was about one room and a small side room," part of the school district's compensation for teaching the 1940-41 year. She had come as a single first-year teacher and taught only that year. After their June 1941 wedding, Dad joined her in the tiny apartment, but they would have to vacate the school's property by September when a new teacher would come to begin the school year.

In their tiny space, with no running water and barely room for two people, they were in no position to provide real hospitality for Grandpa Swearingen, but there he was. "He didn't have a home anymore," Mom explained, "he just went from place to place with his wood-working tools. When he arrived, your dad asked me, 'Has he come to stay?'" expressing his misgivings about Grandpa Swearingen's lifestyle. It didn't meet the expectations of Dad's own family; they always had homes.

One of Mom's cousins later corrected the story for me, saying that Addison Swearingen did indeed have a home with his son Glen in

Centralia, Washington, but that he traveled here and there in South Dakota, Montana, Oregon, and Washington, staying for a while with various members of his extended family. He made them useful things and then moved on. Traditional stories of Johnny Appleseed and his bag of seeds come to mind, but the bag Addison carried was not full of seeds; his contained tools. There was no floor lathe, no drill press, and no electric saw. Electricity would not arrive on the farms and in small towns for many years. But Addison brought the skills and ingenuity to use his crude portable equipment.

Being on the move was nothing new for Addison Swearingen. He had married Sarah Jane (Sadie) Smith in 1890 in Denver, Colorado. Between 1891 and 1917, their eleven children were born in at least four locations: Denver; Lucas, Kansas; Ottumwa, Iowa; and Huron, South Dakota. After Sadie died in 1932 in Sheridan, Wyoming, across the border from their last farm home near Decker, Montana, he lived with his son Glen. Did he, widowed, voluntarily "downsize," as we would say today, or did he lose his home due to the economics of the depression? I assume he retired from farming to have more time to devote to his woodworking, and he turned his farm over to his son. Later they all moved to the Northwest as many others did during that time.

In 1941, Grandpa Swearingen knew that he could be of help to his newly married granddaughter, my mom. Likely he showed up uninvited; perhaps he even surprised my parents. No homes in that part of the country had telephones; they would not come for nearly another twenty years. If he had notified my parents he was coming, it would have been by postcard.

I imagine his arriving on the spur line of the Milwaukee Railroad that connected to the main transcontinental line in Huron, South Dakota, and ran west to Rapid City. If Mom and Dad knew he was coming, they would have met him at the Okaton Depot to give him a ride. If it was a surprise visit, he walked to the front door of the teacherage and knocked.

8

He entered their humble space, and somehow, they found a place for him to sleep. He must have been embarrassed to intrude so intimately on the privacy of the newlyweds, so he looked for another possibility. "There was a little house on the property, too," Mom recalled, as if their half of the teacherage was big! Actually, she spoke of the coal storage shed. One summer day while Mom and Dad were away, they came back to discover that Grandpa Swearingen had moved into the shed. He stayed there until summer was nearly over, and it was time for school to start. In telling her story, Mom did not mention the pressure she and Dad were under to move out of the teacherage before it was needed by a new teacher in September. The house on Dad's farmland still needed reclamation, so they lived for a for a short time in a house in Okaton before they could move into their own place in 1942. But before they left the teacherage, Grandpa Swearingen felt he had done enough for them, so it was time for him to move along.

I do not know all the things Addison Swearingen made for my parents or for others in the community, but Dad's early reluctance to welcome him soon dissipated. Mom remembered, "Dad said Grandpa was the only one around who had tools to make the wooden bearings they needed for a threshing machine." I have no memory of the machines my great-grandpa repaired, but my siblings and I remember well the pieces of his woodwork that became a part of our childhood daily lives. There was a sturdy four-legged stool about a foot tall. Our mother, at five-foot one, always appreciated having a stool nearby to reach things stored high. It was also a convenient seat for a child or for anyone changing shoes. The stool, painted white, was always at hand, and my sister Crystal still uses it in her Oregon home. She also has a newspaper rack Addison made with an artistic star design created by holes drilled in its sides.

We have lost track of a higher stool and a simple wooden bench without a back that stood on legs made of a single board on each end. The bench held tubs of laundry rinse water on wash days, or a number of kids eating at an overflow dinner table when there were guests. My brother Gene tells of a piece of our great-grandpa's work now in his California home, "a beautiful sock darner that he turned on a lathe," so definitely not made in Okaton during the summer of 1941. "The wood is gorgeous," Gene says. "I don't really know what species it is, but I like to think that it is made out of South Dakota cottonwood." Gene inherited it when Mom died, as she had inherited it from our grandmother Crystal Bowder.

The treasure I have is a trivet, but we never called it that; it was just a "hot pad" used in the kitchen. Like Gene, I wonder what species of wood did he use? Apparently, there are about five different kinds. And where did he obtain the material? This simple piece of art is still a constant reminder of my great grandfather.

Even though he had made himself quite useful to my young parents, when it came time for this elderly drifter to move on, both Dad and Mom were probably relieved. But there is a sense in which he was always with us. "Although he died before I was born," my brother Gene writes, "I have always considered him one of my most important role models. As a child I was highly impressed by the household items that he made, and it inspired me to think that I could do that too . . . Following his example, I have always been inclined to make whatever I feel is needed around the house."

I had one opportunity to meet Great-Grandpa Swearingen. In February 1944 when I was one year old, my mother took me by train from South Dakota to Salem, Oregon, to visit the family and to introduce her parents Frank and Crystal Bowder to their first grandson. We took the Great Northern Railroad that stopped in Pierre, South Dakota, on a direct route to the Northwest. Through the years Mom spoke often of this trip. The country was in the midst of World War II, and the trains going in both directions were full of young soldiers traveling to or from assignments. Mother was not shy, and apparently neither was I. She recalled how the soldiers made "a fuss over" me and played with me as I wandered up and down the aisle on the day and a half train ride in each direction.

When we got to my grandparents' home, Grandma's father, Addison Swearingen was there. A four-generation picture, taken in front of a Salem, Oregon, church gives testimony to the fact that we were all together, even though I was too young to remember. A few months later Addison Swearingen died in Centralia, Washington.

At nearly seventy-six years my great grandpa was deaf, but Mom said that he could hear my high-pitched baby laugh. Mom remembered fondly his joy at hearing me. I was an active toddler, unable or unwilling to sit quietly, which he attributed to "wiggle worms" in the drinking water. He must have referred to water drawn directly from the snow and rain-fed stock pond, the dam, near our house. Growing up there I only remember using filtered and chlorinated drinking water delivered by truck from Murdo. My great-grandpa's remarks suggest that early on the family drank untreated water. I have no evidence of the use of such water, and I doubt I would have been given it at my age. But the details did not matter. My great-grandpa, unable to hear, was surely not limited by facts when expressing an opinion or making a joke.

As I look at the four-generation picture, I am reminded that I am the last surviving member of my mother's family who ever met Addison Swearingen. My Aunt Frances Storm, the last of my mother's siblings, died in 2014 at the age of 99, and her two daughters Geri and Linda, the only cousins older than me on the Bowder side of the family, preceded her in death. My next oldest cousin Robert Bowder was born in Salem, Oregon, a few months before our great-grandfather died in Washington.

John Henry Addison Swearingen lives in family legend. I am glad that he came to be a part of my parents' household for a short time and left his legacy in wood. I understand Dad's apprehension about his arrival but share his appreciation of the gifts of this unusual man.

Ed and Margaret (Peggy) Roghair on steps of Okaton teacherage shortly after their marriage in June 1941.

John Henry Addison Swearingen, my great-grandpa.

My mother Margaret wrote on the back of this picture: "Four
Generations: John Henry Addison Swearingen, Crystal Swearingen
Bowder, Margaret Bowder Roghair, James Edward Roghair, 1944"

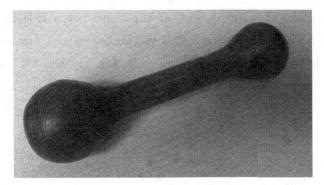

This is a sock darner made by Addison Swearingen that
my brother Gene inherited—a piece he treasures.

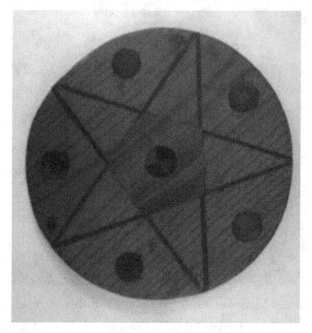

This trivet is a 5¾-inch piece of utilitarian art made by my great-grandpa Addison Swearingen, probably not while he visited my parents Ed and Margaret Roghair in the summer of 1941. A note by my mother pasted to its back says, "Great-Grandpa Swearingen liked to hear baby Jimmy [me] laugh (Feb. '44). He died 4-'44. (Other records indicate he died August 15, 1944, in Centralia, Washington.)

THREE

A Cold Start

One week in January 1943, it was so cold in Jones County, South Dakota, that the nightly low temperatures ranged from minus six to minus thirty degrees Fahrenheit. On two days, the highs did not rise above zero.

That week west of Okaton, on a farm that had no garage, Dad's 1939 Ford sedan would not start. Mom was twenty-six years old and pregnant. She had decided that it was time to go. The Ford was their only vehicle, except for a John Deere Model A tractor that wouldn't start either. There was no one to help. The closest neighbors were half a mile away, and Dad's own family, even farther. There were no telephones.

Dad was not inclined to leave Mom and risk walking for help in the bitter cold, so he used his own ingenuity. He lit a fire on the frozen ground under the car engine, and burning hay warmed it enough to get it running. I never remember seeing my father take such a risk, but I heard this story many times. Perhaps, at age thirty, Dad was youthfully fearless. Maybe he had a guardian angel. There was no explosion, and they were soon on their way.

The original US Highway 16 was nearly one-hundred tedious miles to Chamberlain. Blacktopped a decade or more before World War II, the highway passed through the center of eight little towns and followed the rolling contour of the prairie. It was laid out mostly on the primary compass directions—long straight stretches on section lines a mile apart, interrupted by ninety degree turns. If there was a speed limit, it was not over sixty miles per hour on the open road. But with all the hills, towns, and sharp curves, one could not safely average anywhere near sixty. The trip must have taken at least three hours. Dad persisted, got Mom across the bridge over the Missouri River, and they eventually arrived at their destination.

In my imagination I see Dad calmly preparing for this trip and driving the long distance. He was persistent, unruffled, and capable in the face of any distraction. He could improvise a solution to any problem and do whatever needed to be done—survival traits acquired growing up on isolated farms, first in northwest Iowa and then near Okaton. He was used to consistently dealing with the vagaries of unpredictable people, weather, crops, machines, animals, and income. He had developed a laid-back personal style that served him well in his sixty-five-year marriage with Mom.

Mom's experience and personality were quite different from Dad's. She had grown up in the small town of Timber Lake, South Dakota, wedged between two Indian reservations. Her father, Frank Bowder, operated a general store, traded for furs, bought cream to send off to Minneapolis on the Milwaukee Railroad, and sold almost anything needed in the town. Her mother, Crystal, cared for the family of nine children and took in strangers who needed a place to stay. It was not a life of luxury, but it was always filled with a bustle of human activity.

The isolation of farm life and the patience it required were new to Mom. She and Dad had moved into an abandoned farmhouse and worked hard to make it a home, but she expected life to move at her pace. Sometimes it didn't. I can imagine her impatient interaction with Dad as he worked to start the car, to pack what was needed, and then to drive to Chamberlain. Likely she had never traveled that road before since she had lived in the area for only two years. I can hear her asking Dad repeatedly how much farther it was—urging him on, but then warning him, "Ed, don't take the curves so fast." This trip, like many things in their marriage, would pit Mom's impatience against Dad's calm confidence.

Actually, I do not really know the time of day or the details of the trip—and now there is no one to ask. I have always imagined the tale of this frigid beginning to my story as a time of frenzy set in the dead of night when the temperatures were the coldest. Surely Mom's contractions had not yet begun, although my birth was imminent. Maybe the trip had been planned in advance to get Mom to a private home near the hospital where she would board while awaiting the time of delivery.

The long car trip to Chamberlain is also what I imagine. But of course, it may be that they were catching the eastbound Milwaukee train in Okaton or Murdo and had only a few miles to drive. In that case the urgency would have been to arrive at the train station on time. Notes Dad wrote for *Dakota Roghairs* mention his trying to get to Chamberlain by train to visit us in the hospital after my birth. When the train failed to stop in Okaton, he drove the thirteen miles to Murdo, beat the train, and boarded there. He was always quick to solve a problem.

The hospital in Pierre would have been about an hour less driving time, although it was not available by rail since it was on a different line. None of the Roghairs in my Dad's generation, or any of my four older Roghair cousins, had been born in a hospital. There surely were midwives in the Okaton area. But in my childhood, I never heard a word about these local women or their work. It was not discussed in the presence of children—at least not the boys.

My parents had chosen Chamberlain Sanitarium (the hospital) because Dad's sister Harriet was a nurse there. Aunt Harriet's position began a new family precedent, and later that year my cousin Alice Mae was also born in Chamberlain rather than at home as her older siblings had been. Using Harriet's hospital was a matter of family loyalty.

I was born on January 30, 1943. After the customary days of bed rest for Mom, on my eleventh day, we were released from the hospital. The trip home was surely more relaxed than the trip out—which must have been a relief for Dad. Having just made several trips between home and the hospital to look after his wife and son, while still caring for the farm animals at home, he was ready for a more routine domestic life. And now, Mom's attention wasn't on the road; she was occupied with caring for her first-born. The proud parents stopped at Grandpa and Grandma Roghair's home to show off the newest member of the family before making the final few miles of their trip home. Thus began my adventures on the farm.

Of course, I don't remember anything of my first two years except the stories my parents told. One incident they especially liked to relate happened when I was one year old. I couldn't keep any food in my stomach. I didn't seem to be ill in any other way but vomited every time I ate. They were puzzled and only understood what had been wrong when I finally threw up a small chicken feather that had escaped from my pillow. Mom cleaned that feather and put it in my baby book, a remembrance of the mysterious ailment that had baffled my young parents.

My earliest memory is receiving the card from my mother for my second birthday. She was boarding at a private home near the hospital in Pierre awaiting the birth of my brother Gene. My aunt Harriet had moved on from Chamberlain, so the hospital in Pierre was the choice.

With Gene's arrival, my parents were mastering the art of parenting—and no more hay was burned under the car.

James Edward Roghair, 1 week old
with Aunt Harriet.

Ed, Peggy, and baby
Jimmy going home.

The hospital in Chamberlain where Harriet
worked and where Jim was born.

PART B

A Biography of Our Okaton Home

FOUR

Making a House a Home

Reclaiming a House

An abandoned house stood three and a half miles northwest of Okaton, South Dakota, on farmland my father had acquired before my parents' wedding, and they were to move into it. Mother had been living in half of the teacherage, and Dad moved in with her after their marriage in June. I had always assumed they prepared and moved into their *new* home during that first summer. But summers were busy with the preparation for planting next year's crop, the current wheat harvest in July, and then early fall sowing of the new crop. I had often wondered how they had readied their farmhouse and moved in by September, when the school would need the teacherage for another teacher.

Rereading Dad's contribution to *Dakota Roghairs*, I discovered what he had written or likely dictated to Mother: "We were married on June 8, 1941. We lived in the west half of the Okaton teacherage a while, then moved to the Lobdell place. The cistern had rusted out and mice lived in it, so I carried some water from the railroad cistern. Early in 1942 we moved to the Wilsey place, one of the first two story houses around the area."

At that time the various places were designated by the names of the original homesteaders. The actual Lobdell homestead was in the eastern part of the county, near Draper. But shortly after the homesteading period, Don Lobdell had purchased a ranch several miles south of Okaton on the White River flood plain. It was the place where we had later known three generations of the Graham family to live, and we had visited them frequently while we were growing up. My siblings and I are sure that if our parents had lived in either of the two houses on that ranch, we would have heard our parents mention it. So, after conferring with the Lobdells' grandson, Wayne Arp, only a few years older than I, I have concluded that Mom and Dad must have moved into an unoccupied house in the town of Okaton for a few months. The house was owned by the Lobdells, who later moved into it in 1945 at the end of WWII. They had lived in Oregon during the war. Living in town our parents began the long process of reclaiming the house on their own land to make it their home.

Lovingly built a generation or so earlier by someone unknown to us, this house had most recently been used as a granary. The young couple worked hard to clean it, to put up wallpaper in each of the four first-floor rooms, to reduce the mouse population, and to prepare a vegetable garden. Ready or not, Mom and Dad had moved into it before I was born in January 1943. But the reclaiming, repairing, and improving continued for the fifteen years they lived there. They welcomed each of us children into it as we arrived: after I was born, came Gene in February 1945; Crystal (Crysti), July 1947; and Wallace (Wally), May 1952. We each had our own part in making it home. In the early 1950s we were still trying to keep down the mouse population. Using wooden snap traps, I received a nickel for each one I caught.

Dad's description of it as a two-story house makes it sound larger than it really was. It was tiny—probably less than twenty by forty feet. The first floor had four little rooms and an enclosed, but unheated, back porch half the length of the house. Two partially finished attic rooms comprised the second floor, the pitched roof being the side walls of the larger room with a window at the south end. The smaller room had short side walls and a window at the opposite end. There were storage areas under the roof on two sides of the smaller room. Below the house was an unfinished earthen cellar. The growing family eventually expanded into the whole house.

The Origins of the House

Little did we consider the origins of our house. It wasn't until the 1980s that I learned some of its story. After we had departed in 1957, another family occupied it for several years, and it was again abandoned. Then my cousin Henry Roghair acquired the property and built a new house for his family. As he deconstructed our little house, he discovered evidence of its origin. The lumber used to build it was not uniform. Its oddly matched materials revealed that it had been constructed from precious wood salvaged from several claim shanties.

Such shanties were built in 1906 as settlers poured into the area, most aboard the newly completed Milwaukee Railroad Black Hills spur line. They came to claim land offered by the Homestead Act of 1862, passed by Congress and signed by President Lincoln after the secession of the Confederate States. The 1906 homesteading in western South Dakota was, however, clearly an abrogation of the 1886 Treaty of Fort Laramie that had granted the Lakota and Dakota tribes all of the land in what is now South Dakota west of the Missouri River. By then, settlers had already eagerly claimed millions of acres of tribal land in other areas of the continent, and homesteading in South Dakota continued that process.

Anyone at least twenty-one years old or head of a household, who was a citizen or an applicant for citizenship, could file a claim for 160 acres—a quarter section (one-fourth of a square mile). The initial filing fee was $18.00, but to "prove up" the ownership was a bit more costly. The homesteader was required to build a house at least ten by fourteen feet (the shanty), live on the land five years without absence of more than six months per year, and cultivate at least ten acres. With the testimony of two neighbors that the requirements had been met, the land was "proved up," and the new owner gained title. An alternate process was to live on the land for six months and then buy it for $1.25 per acre, a total of $200.00. (The 1906 cost may seem unbelievably low, but an Internet site conveniently converted the values into 2021 dollars, showing more clearly the real significance of the investment: in 2021 dollars the $18 filing fee would be $534; the $1.25 per acre, almost $30; and the $200 buy-out, almost $6,000.)

The cold winters, hot summers, shallow topsoil, and dry conditions made it impossible to make a living farming such small plots. Many settlers gave up and abandoned their claims, or they stayed six months and then sold the land to pay off their $200.00 as soon as possible. Of course, some hardy souls stayed and began piecing together ever-larger farms.

In 1925 my grandparents Henry and Cornelia Roghair arrived in Okaton from northwest Iowa with their eight children, "two and a half dozen," as Grandma told her new neighbors. They originally purchased a homestead of 160 acres with a tiny house—a kitchen with an attic above and a lean-to room. Grandpa and his sons laid a foundation and began to expand the structure. He also started acquiring additional farmland to buy or rent.

Seventeen years later, when my parents moved onto Dad's farm it consisted of three contiguous quarters of land northwest of Okaton and two additional quarters several miles to the east, 800 acres in all. It was not a large farm, even in the 1940s, although Dad's land had been homesteaded by five separate owners in 1906. The building materials of our modest house became a silent memorial to the five claim shanties that had been on Dad's farmland and many others that had once dotted the landscape. My parents were focused on the future—making the house the best home they could. Did my parents think about—or even know—how their residence represented the shanties of the past?

Our Home's Landscape

Although most farmhouses in our community were designed and built with front doors, no one used them. The customary farm driveway and a well-worn path led to the back door. Visitors entered houses through the kitchen. But Mom was determined that her home have a welcoming front door. When Dad built a fence around our house, he placed an attractive unpainted wooden gate at the front, and later laid a concrete sidewalk up to the front door.

Mom planted a row of hardy Russian olive trees on either side of the straight, flat driveway coming in from the dirt township road. The drive curved slightly in front of the house and ended in a graceful circle on the side of a hill just above the front door. There was no pavement or gravel, just the common dark gumbo which turned into extraordinarily sticky mud when wet. But it was usually dry and packed hard. Although our parents probably didn't consider it when they moved in, there was a value to the sloping driveway for growing children. We discovered that when learning to ride a bicycle, we could coast down the gentle slope past the house and all the way to the barn, while concentrating on balance, without having to learn to pedal at the same time.

My parents planted a Chinese elm a few feet north of the front gate, spearmint on either side of the front door, and a native wild rose—yellow instead of the usual pink—at the southeast corner of the house. These plants welcomed visitors, as Mom had hoped, and grew without much special attention. There was no front porch; our door opened directly into a tiny square hallway that led to the living room.

The Dam and Water

The most distinctive feature of our farm's landscape was water. Dad had added a dam to what would have been a powder-dry draw most of the year and a raging stream during spring snowmelt or after a heavy downpour. About the time they moved in, Dad hired someone with dirt-moving equipment to gouge out an area to hold water and to make an embankment from the removed dirt. We called both the earthwork and the artificial lake behind it the *dam*. So instead of a dry creek, the view in two directions below our house and near the barn to the west was a beautiful pond. Each year in the spring and early summer, southeast of the house at the upper end of the dam, cattails and willows grew with their feet in water until it receded later in the season.

The cattails were special—an intentional improvement. When we were children, a few times a year, the family made a shopping trip to Pierre, South Dakota, seventy-five miles away. Once, about halfway home, Mom asked Dad to stop the car and walk down through tall grass to someone else's dam to pick a few cattail heads. He brought them home, and on a windy day, Dad stood in front of the house, near the slope down to the dam, and "fuzzed" the cattails. After that we had cattails every year.

The dam was a stock pond, and our few cows did drink there, even in the cold of winter when we had to chop a hole in the ice each day for them. Water pumped from the dam irrigated our vegetable garden. We could even swim in the dam in the summer, although it was not an ideal swimming pool—always muddy underfoot and full of water-loving weeds. It was also a place to play in the winter, but not an ideal ice rink, either. Usually, it froze with an uneven surface because of the ever-present wind. It was, however, a wonderful haven for ducks most of the year. We had a small flock of white, domestic Chinese ducks who did not fly but mingled with the wild Mallards when they came. The ducks were always looking for a meal of insects or small fish. Although he didn't care to fish himself,

Dad must have stocked the dam with bullheads, bass, and sunfish. Still, I always had the idea that birds had dropped the fish in the water for us.

Although my parents may have used the dam as a source of drinking water in the very beginning, I have no knowledge of that. All water I remember being used in our home came from the filtration plant in Murdo, the county seat, about fifteen miles away. When asked by visitors, unfamiliar with our topography, why we didn't have a well, Dad's answer was the same as his neighbors', "It's easier to drive ten miles for water than to go down ten miles." If there was an aquifer below us, it was very deep and impractical to use. Our trucked-in, chlorinated water was stored in an underground cistern of galvanized steel that held several hundred gallons. Its tight-fitting, lightweight cover was only removed to check the level or to add water. Though a neighbor had a water delivery business, eventually Dad bought a large water tank that he could place on the bed of the farm truck when it was time to get water from Murdo. It was the same truck he used to transport wheat or animals.

Barn and Outbuildings

Of the several outbuildings on our place, the pit toilet was nearest the house. A small chicken coop not far from it was usually occupied by a few hens who gave us eggs and were butchered for meat. The nearby old shed contained Dad's workbench, a hand-powered, wall-mounted drill press, and other tools. Dad always purchased quality tools to be able to maintain the house and the farm machinery.

The shed held some mystery for us. One day there Gene and I managed to capture a small bat with our bare hands. To Mom's consternation, we took it to show her. It got loose and flew around in the house getting us in trouble. Part of the shed's mystery was its original purpose. It might have served as a residence, but we remember it as about ready to fall in. After Dad hired help to build a garage near the driveway, the shed was torn down.

Our barn wasn't very large and usually had a stack of loose (unbaled) hay in front of it. Our herd of cattle was only about twelve or fifteen white-face Herefords and one milk cow. Dad called her Jersey, although she was a Jersey/Guernsey mix. The cows spent most of their time grazing in a pasture near the barn or in one more distant, reached by going under a small wooden bridge on the township road. Most of them stayed out for the summer, only coming to the barn when it stormed. We gave them hay near the barn in winter. Most of the year, Jersey had to come in twice a day to be milked. She stood in one of a row of stanchions and always got some oats or milo to munch while she was there. Whoever was milking held the milk pail between his legs while balancing on the one-legged stool. She was usually docile, but we had to be careful, because Jersey could kick the bucket and waste the day's product. Dad did the milking until Gene and I were old enough to take our turns.

The residents of our farmyard and pasture were often in flux. Cats and a dog were constant, but one day Dad brought home an old horse named Boots, a *plug,* he called her. She joined the cattle in the pasture and wasn't expected to work very hard. She was really a pet. She didn't come with a saddle, so we rode her bareback. Gene spent many hours of a summer or two with a couple of neighbor friends riding around the community on their horses.

Another time, Dad brought home two young pigs. Remembering his childhood experiences on a northwest-Iowa hog farm, he wanted his children to have a similar memory. But what he said to us was, "I wanted you to learn that pigs are bigger than tomcats." They took up residence in a small area in the front of the barn, separate from the cattle. Gene and I were given responsibility for caring for them daily until they were big enough to sell. We then got the sale money to put in our savings accounts, "for college." Although hogs weren't an ongoing part of our menagerie, Dad did later buy a pregnant sow, and we had the new experience of the arrival and raising of baby pigs.

The last arrivals to our farm before we moved were five *bum lambs*. The sheep farmer gave them away because their mothers couldn't care for them. Perhaps they were born to an inexperienced mother who hadn't learned to care for a baby, or more likely, to one who had twins but could only manage one. Like the pigs before them, the sheep got the special place in the front of the barn. They were bottle-fed until they were big enough to eat grass or grain and to run around wherever they pleased.

Two of the lambs were male. When they were still small, Dad had put heavy rubber bands around their testicles to castrate them and keep them from growing into aggressive rams. But for one of them the fix didn't take. As he grew up, he began to chase and butt our four-year old brother Wally, who remembers vividly his fear of that animal. The sheep, like most of the animals who came from time to time, were like pets rather than animals to be butchered for our own use. So, they were eventually sold. The young ram was, however, butchered. But Mom didn't have much experience cooking mutton, and when she boiled it to make a soup, we could hardly eat it because of the strong lanolin taste. It was many years before I voluntarily chose to eat any meat from a sheep.

A short distance from the barn was a wooden granary used exclusively for animal feed, mainly oats and milo (a sorghum). Our cash crop, wheat, was stored in another wooden granary, consisting of two storage bins, at the end of the driveway and across the township road. It was later complemented by a round corrugated steel bin which Gene and I were privileged to help assemble.

On a family farm there was always a variety of things to do and learn, and we were seldom bored. During the fifteen years my parents lived in the little house, they continued to improve it and its surroundings. They succeeded in making it a home we would remember for the rest of our lives.

FIVE

Fences

Dad often told me the story of making the fence around our house and my reactions to it. He described me as a one-year-old watching and trying to help as he worked. He made postholes with a hand-held auger and pulled out the loose dirt, gumbo, with a two-handled posthole digger. He saw me watch him place the wooden posts in their holes, align them to stand straight, shovel in the gumbo, tamp it down with a long steel bar and finally tramp it by foot so the posts were firmly in place.

He placed the steel posts more quickly, driving them in using a steel driver—a tool made of a heavy pipe about four inches in diameter and three feet long with a cover welded to one end. It slipped down over a steel post, and the force of slamming it down onto the post gave a musical ring each time. The posts were soon in place. The fencing material was "hog wire," about four feet high and woven more closely at the bottom than the top. It was attached to the posts with staples hammered into the wood and wire fasteners wound around the steel posts. The woven wire was made taut and held in place by braced wooden posts in the four corners, and the steel posts were at intervals along all sides.

Dad made gates that opened onto front and back paths—slatted, unpainted wood like a picket fence. They were handsome and serviceable but not ostentatious. A larger gate at the side was made of the fence wire to open initially for trucks delivering water and coal, but later stove oil and propane as well. Dad built this fence for keeping things out and for keeping a little boy in. In my memory it was always there.

Dad's fence was a significant contribution to my parents' reclamation of the old house and making it a home. It was prudent protection against the hazards of the vast rural landscape with long distances between farms and many acres of grass, weeds, and crops taller than a toddler in which a child could get lost. Another tempting hazard was the dam, easily accessible to the house, several feet deep, and with mud of a consistency to trap a child at its edges and under the water. Although the fence couldn't prevent the rare visit of rattlesnakes, it provided enough protection that I could safely play outside without Mom's watching me every moment.

Small as I was while observing him making the fence, Dad said I acted like his assistant, or at least his companion. He knew that I didn't understand the real purpose of the fence, and he saw my surprise and disappointment when I realized that it locked me in. Even though I can't consciously remember the project, I don't recall any fence being a barrier between Dad and me. His early acts of unspoken love and duty were a prelude to other fence-making opportunities we were to share.

When I was about nine, old enough to actually help build a fence, it was to enlarge our pasture. This fence was of much simpler construction than the first one, just two strands of barbed wire. The upper one was attached to the posts with porcelain insulators and to a battery-powered, low-voltage charger that emitted a shock every few seconds—enough to discourage the cows from getting out. The lower strand was grounded directly to steel posts set in the dirt.

The comradery I felt as we worked on the project was more mature than my feelings as a toddler. Sometimes we were together and sometimes at considerable distance from each other, but always we were making something to view proudly for years to come. Dad was skilled at laying out a fence without the aid of any surveying equipment; he could eyeball it accurately. Holding a strategically placed steel post, I stood a hundred yards away—too far to hear Dad's words, but as he pointed to the right or the left, I moved the post to its exact location. It was an important responsibility.

I enjoyed working where we could hear the wild birds and see the blooming flowers. But the singing of the steel post driver placing its claim on the prairie gumbo became a surprising physics lesson I would only understand later. I observed a significant delay between seeing the driver hit the post and hearing its sound. It was of course delayed because the speed of sound is much slower than the speed of light, a phenomenon I wouldn't understand until later.

The fence we made that year added safety and value to our farm, but its importance for me was the opportunity to learn and work with Dad more intimately than in ordinary daily activities. Years later I considered the significance of those experiences with him. I was thirty years old living in inner city Cincinnati, hundreds of miles from my prairie home and worlds away from my childhood life. My first son was born on a Sunday morning. I left him and his mother in the hospital and went to the church where I was associate pastor. With no responsibility that day, but full of emotions I sat in the pew. My thoughts went back to fence-making with my dad two decades earlier. How could I, living and working in an urban environment, provide my new son experiences as precious as those my father had given me? A tear came to my eye. After the service an older woman who sat nearby saw on my face what was in my mind and said, "It is an experience when you become a parent, isn't it?" How right she was.

I never felt that I could offer my own sons childhood experiences as precious as those I had with my dad. Mowing a lawn or raking leaves in the city never seemed to arouse in my children the sense of commonly held value and purpose that sharing farm work with Dad had for me. But I hope there were things we did together that they remember with as much gratitude as I have for spending time making fences with Dad.

SIX

Chic Sale

The outhouse was a daily part of our family experience. Summer and winter, whether the outside temperature was 100°F or -30°F—man, woman, or child—we all made our way to the little structure and sat on one of its wooden seats. In winter there was frigid, tactile encouragement to get done quickly; in the heat of summer, there were the flies, wasps, and aroma. But it was always our place. The nighttime option beside the bed was an enameled steel chamber pot with a lid. It was never used during the day, and anytime it was used, it required prompt attention the next day. Failure to take care of it risked daytime spill emergencies in the tiny bedroom or a smell if left more than a day. Normally it was best to go outside day or night.

I reflect on the striking differences between my childhood experiences and the common daily life I share with many others in the twenty-first century. Recently in a museum I saw the crudely crafted wheel of a nineteenth century oxcart cut from the cross-section of a tree trunk and patched somewhere *en route* when a piece broke off. I mused aloud on how it would be to travel on such a conveyance. A youthful stranger answered, "I prefer to fly, myself," and she added, "I like running water and bathrooms, too."

Every morning I go into my bathroom, sit down on a comfortable seat, and do what has to be done. I am always relieved and deeply thankful that my aging digestive system is still working. But there is more to it; daily I am reminded of how things were in times gone by.

In my fourteen years on the farm, the toilet, as we called our outhouse, did not always seem uncomfortable. I spent time on the seat looking at the ever-present, outdated Sears Roebuck, Montgomery Ward, and Spiegel catalogues. We did have rolls of toilet paper, so the catalogues were only an emergency backup. But they were also a traditional throwback to the time when they were the only option people had. I found the pages educational. They were an opportunity to privately study pictures of the women's underwear and diagrams for fitting bras. Of course, the catalogues went far beyond pre-adolescent prurient curiosity to include almost anything needed on the farm.

A trip to the toilet after dark could sometimes be a little scary, especially when we had heard a radio news report that a prison escapee might be loose in our area. Our home was remote, more than half a mile from any other house and even farther from a paved highway, but I could imagine this guy shooting at me in the dark, even though I knew it was unlikely. I wasn't frightened enough to avoid going to the toilet by myself, and I certainly didn't tell anyone about my fears. But I do remember running to the toilet a bit more quickly during that scare.

Later a rumor was started by a rancher in the area who claimed to have seen a mountain lion. That brought some consternation to our family, but I remember Dad dismissing the story to a neighbor by saying that guy was "always a-lyin' down on his place." It brought a chuckle to Dad's friend. Nevertheless, that night I again ran to and from the toilet a little faster than usual.

Outhouse emergencies did occasionally occur. For most nighttime activities before we got electricity, the family shared only two flashlights, each powered by two D Cell batteries. We did carry a kerosene lantern to the barn if we were late milking the cow, but a flashlight always accompanied us to the toilet. Occasionally one of the kids would carelessly drop the light into the pit. It was a catastrophe that called for immediate action. We had to get the other flashlight to see what we were doing, then find the garden hoe and dip it into the cavity to retrieve the light from the filth. We had to clean it immediately before we could put it back into service. Flashlights were not considered disposable.

When the toilet's pit was too full Dad hired a man to help him move it. By hand they dug a new pit about four-by-four feet and five feet deep. I was in school and didn't help with the digging or the actual move. The toilet and its concrete slab floor were pulled by farm tractor to the new pit, and wooden planks were placed over the new hole to keep the slab from falling in while it was being placed. When it was set, the family soon became accustomed to walking ten or fifteen yards west instead of south from our back door, and the next year weeds grew tall over the old pit.

Our toilet was more sophisticated than those of our neighbors. It had a corrugated, galvanized steel roof that slanted down from front to back, and wooden siding painted white to match our house. Inside were two wooden seats—large and small. Each was mounted on a carefully constructed hollow platform and each had a hinged wooden lid. They also had hinged seats that could be raised to prevent male users from getting the seats wet. Many farm toilets were unpainted and appeared to have been haphazardly nailed together. Their holes were just cut into a board with no lids or seats to raise and no concrete floor. Ours was clearly made by an experienced carpenter. Perhaps it had originally been in use at a public building in the area.

I thought I once heard Dad say something about our toilet being a "Chick toilet." I had assumed he spoke of its unusual construction—perhaps it was named for a carpenter or designer named Chick. But after the intervening years, when I began to write this story, and long after it was too late to ask my father about it, I began to investigate. On the internet I only found pornography when I looked up "Chick Toilets." Pursuing the subject further I discovered Charles (Chic) Sale, born in Huron in 1885 about four years before South Dakota statehood. He and my Grandpa Bowder, slightly younger, surely knew each other as children.

Chic Sale became a vaudeville and silent movie comedian. He created a stage character named Lem Putt, an Urbana, Illinois, carpenter who specialized in building outhouses. Chic Sale was an early Rotary Club member, and he visited clubs in towns wherever he performed professionally. He did his Lem Putt routine for the clubs. Over and over, he told audiences straight-facedly the details of how to build the perfect outhouse. His sketch became so popular that other comedians began stealing his material.

Chic Sale eventually wrote up his spiel and published it in 1929 as *The Specialist*, a twenty-six-page bestseller that is still in print. His wit and humor made him so popular he took off half a year to answer his fan mail, and a fellow comedian, Groucho Marx, made Chic the butt of his jokes.

He was disconcerted when his character became so popular in the 1930s and 40s that outhouses all over the world had "Chic Sale" signs on them. His name became a slang term for toilets themselves. Finally, I understood that Dad was calling our toilet a Chic Sale. It had nothing to do with its design or construction; Dad was simply in tune with the jargon of his generation.

Our toilet was always an important part of daily life. I didn't think of our family as deprived, and I don't look back on the time as distasteful. Things simply were what they were. I am, however, daily grateful for the conveniences I now know, and I agree with the woman I met in the museum: I prefer airplanes to oxcarts and running water and bathrooms to the alternatives.

SEVEN

Life in Our Kitchen

Mom was successful in her determination that the front door of our house be its primary entrance, so visitors did not regularly enter our house through the kitchen door. But, as in neighboring farm homes, the kitchen was still the center of activity. Much in our house changed over the years—but never the location of its center.

Typical of farm homes in the area, ours did not have the luxury of a separate dining room, even though eating together daily was a significant part of our lives. The kitchen was long and narrow with bright green leafy wallpaper and a white ceiling. At one end stood the simple wooden kitchen table, painted white and covered with red checkered oilcloth. Six matching white wooden chairs could easily fit around the table, but often a highchair took the place of one of them when a baby was added to our number. The family gathered three times a day without fail. When the farming occasionally required Dad to work into the night, his supper was held for him, but the rest of us ate together.

Ordinarily Dad sat at the south end near the window and Mom at the other end closer to the cook stove. We children sat along the sides in assigned places that changed from time to time. Leaves were added to lengthen the table when company came. That made the room cramped, but guests were always welcome.

Dad usually gave a long and comprehensive blessing at the beginning of the meal. Long prayers were a trait he shared with his own father; Mom's were shorter. Reading from the Bible or a Bible story book came at the end of one meal every day. Dad read through *Hurlbut's Story of the Bible* and another children's Bible book. More than once, he read the entire Bible out loud from cover to cover, one chapter a day—that was a project that took more than three years. After the Revised Standard Version came out in 1952, he read from it instead of the King James. We came to know the Bible stories well. But hearing every chapter was at times tedious—even meaningless—to youngsters.

The last thing before anyone was excused from the table was a prayer of thanksgiving offered by one of us children. We had all memorized several prayers, but the one we used most often has been said by countless numbers of American children:

> *Thank you for the world so sweet.*
> *Thank you for the food we eat.*
> *Thank you for the birds that sing.*
> *Thank you, God, for everything. Amen.*

Having prayed, we were off to our play or work. But that normally began with clearing the table and washing, rinsing, and drying the dishes before putting them back on the shelves. At times we would race to the sink to claim the job of washing the dishes, because whoever washed was finished first.

The kitchen table was a place where many things were done besides eating. It was for recreation—we played board games, including Uncle Wiggly, checkers, and Chinese checkers and card games like 500, Rook and whist. We acquired a Scrabble game and enjoyed it, but never got a Monopoly set, so we had to be satisfied to play that game at the homes of our cousins or friends. When we got a ping pong set, we attached its net to the table when we wanted to play. Handicraft and other 4-H projects were accomplished there. Our kitchen table was the primary place for much of our family's daily activity.

Beyond the kitchen table was a white corner cupboard for china. It had glass doors that displayed the Fiestaware settings used daily: two sizes of plates, soup bowls, cups, and saucers all in bright green, orange, yellow, blue and a cream color. There were matching salt and pepper shakers, a cream pitcher, and a sugar bowl. A few other serving dishes and trays were also stored there. On the wall near the ceiling, between the cupboard and the window, hung a small glossy plaque with gilt-edged black letters and tiny flowers on a dark background with a prayer, "God Bless our Home"—a cherished wedding gift.

Through the south window, especially in spring, we might see a red-winged blackbird sitting on a corner fence post. Its distinctive bright red and yellow markings set off its jet-black body—a beautiful bird. The blackbirds seemed to enjoy being near human habitation. From the same window in summer, we could glimpse the tops of red hollyhocks peeking over the windowsill, and further out, a row of large deep purple irises blooming beside the dirt path. These species, like those in the front, seemed to thrive on neglect. Scraping a livelihood out of the poor ground with sparse precipitation, our family did not commit much energy to pampering its flowers.

When evening came, Mom or Dad carefully placed the kerosene Aladdin Lamp on the kitchen table and lit it with a wooden kitchen match. Its white porcelain base contained the fuel. Its silk mantle and circular wick below were enclosed in a tall, slim, clear glass chimney. The lamp gave a characteristic white light, cool and soothing, much brighter than the yellowish glow of the common kerosene lamps used by most of our neighbors and in the rest of our house. When this precious lamp was moved into the living room, one of our parents carried it. I was certainly proud to have such a bright light in our home—maybe we all were.

The end of the kitchen opposite the table was a working area. Counters and cupboards just beyond the table and at the other end of the room held pots, pans, and other cooking and baking necessities. On the inside wall sat the kitchen range that burned either wood or coal, its pipe attached to the brick chimney in the center of the house. The range gave warmth to the house and kept the kitchen comfortable in winter but made it terribly hot in the summer. In time, this range was replaced by a bottled gas (propane) stove. The old one was moved to the back porch and continued to be used to heat laundry water. The porch had previously been unheated. For the new range two upright containers of propane were placed north of the house. They were replaced in a few years by a larger container about fifteen feet long. Cooking with the gas burners and oven took less time and effort than using the old range.

Mom worked hard in the kitchen to provide three good meals every day and to preserve summer produce for the winter. We thought of her as a master chef. If there was a community potluck, we kids always wanted Mom to bring her potato salad. She used boiled eggs, mayonnaise, yellow mustard, and dill as ingredients. We didn't think any other cook's potato salad could match hers—we didn't even want to try anyone else's.

Cooking, especially baking in the coal fired oven, was something Mom had to learn after her marriage. I don't know what Grandma Bowder's kitchen was like when Mom was growing up, but it seems that Grandma hadn't given her daughters much culinary opportunity before they were on their own. After her marriage Mom tried to get recipes from her mother-in-law, Grandma Roghair, to make sure she could prepare what my dad liked. But she didn't find Grandma's advice very helpful; nothing was written down. Mom remembered, "She just said to add a little of this and a little of that, and I didn't know how to do it."

But Mom did learn, and we ate well. In the summer we had fresh vegetables from the garden and in the winter, those that had been canned.

We had home-grown chicken, pork, beef, whole raw milk, home-churned butter, and home-made bread, cookies, and cake. We always had more than enough. Mom was, also, especially attentive to leftovers. Nothing went to waste, and she kept serving something until it was finally used up. Her persistence in the kitchen paid off; in her senior years, she entered recipe contests and won prizes for what she had concocted.

The kitchen sink was across the narrow room from the range, against the outside wall and near the door to the back porch. Since there was no running water, a hand pump on the end of the sink counter brought water in from the cistern. When the long handle was raised the leather plunger went down, then a push of the handle drew the water up. It gushed out. Used often, the pump stayed primed most of the time, and with a swing or two of the arm a wash basin or a tea kettle would be filled. It didn't take much effort to fill the white enamel cup we all drank from. A shared towel hung on the end of the sink.

A five-gallon grease pail, emptied after lubricating farm machinery, became the slop bucket serving as the drain under the sink. It caught any water that couldn't be used again in the house to be dumped on an outdoor plant or taken to the pigs. The bucket under the sink was eventually replaced by a cesspool. Dad hired a neighbor to help him to hand-dig into the gumbo and the shale beneath. A pipe from the sink went down into the cellar under the house, out under the ground of the back yard, down the hill, under the clothesline and into the new cesspool. The excavation was about five feet square and five feet deep. The lining and covering were made of two-inch thick wooden planks. There was no pump or leach field; the wastewater would dissipate into the nearby ground. Another improvement accomplished.

Like the table, the kitchen sink served many purposes. It was where we did all of our hand washing, until Mom placed a basin on a small table on the back porch especially for use when we were coming in with greasy hands. At the sink dishes were done after every meal. Vegetables and fruit were washed there. Every night before we went to bed, we stood there to wash our arms, faces, necks and behind our ears—as Mom always reminded us. There we brushed our teeth, but in warm weather we went outdoors to spit toothpaste on the ground. Dad shaved there on Saturday nights. All hot water needed at the sink was heated in a teakettle on the range across from the sink.

From time to time, we spent a day butchering chickens—a dozen or so at a time. Most of the project was done in and around the sink. My brother Gene worked with Dad outdoors to do the first part—to either chop off the heads with an ax or wring the necks. I never wanted to do that part. We doused the chicken carcasses in boiling water before plucking the feathers. We learned the appropriate butcher knife cuts, so the pieces of meat came out in the customary shapes. We children were involved in this process as soon as we were able, but we were never present for the butchering of larger animals.

Next to the range and across from the sink, a door opened into a small pantry where shelves held a few canned goods near the top of the cellar stairs. The unimproved dirt cellar under the house stayed cool in the summer but did not freeze in winter. Shelves of home-canned vegetables and meat, and cases of commercially canned fruit were on shelves at the bottom of the stairs and not far from the set of three large wet-cell batteries connected to the six-volt Wincharger. After a floor furnace replaced the older heating stove in the living room, the furnace became a visible presence hanging from the ceiling of the cellar below the doorway between the kitchen and living room.

The kitchen door next to the sink opened onto the back porch which was completely enclosed but unheated until the coal-burning range was moved there. The porch ran along half the back of the house. It was an addition that Dad constructed shortly after he and Mom moved in. Early in their life together and late one night, Dad heard a strong gust of wind and a crashing sound. He knew immediately what it was. He didn't awaken Mom and didn't even get up to see what had happened. There was nothing to do until morning, so he went back to sleep. When he awoke, he found there had been a small tornado. Timbers of what had been a small back porch had been blown in several directions. His new project was to replace it, and he did.

The prominent feature of our back porch became the Maytag wringer washing machine. It was powered by a two-cycle gasoline engine and started with a foot pedal, similar to those on contemporary motorcycles. Once it was going, it had to run until Mom was finished with it for the day. It took more strength to start than Mom could muster, so Dad did it before he went off to do his farm work. The Maytag was a roaring presence—like a motorcycle at full speed—for hours through the many loads of wash. The machine stood near the only window on the enclosed porch, and a flexible steel exhaust tube went through a hole in the sash. At the end of the day, through a smaller hole a garden hose drained the water onto a lucky cottonwood in the back yard. The porch was used in the heat of summer and the sub-zero days of winter.

On Monday washdays, the central part of the kitchen, between the table and the cook stove, became the staging area. Mom sorted the laundry into piles to be washed in order. Using the same water all day, she started with the whites, moved through light and dark colored things, and ended with the denim overalls and jeans. While she was sorting, water was heating on the range in two lightweight ten-gallon boilers, one of copper and one of another lightweight metal. Since the range was kept hot for the wash and rinse water, the usual washday noon meal was simmering there as well, navy bean soup. Although I love bean soup today, I hated that soup and would only eat it smothered in ketchup. I think I inherited that taste from my dad; that's the only way he ate the beans.

47

After the loads of clothes were washed, rinsed in a tub of water, and run through the Maytag's wringer, they were hung on steel clotheslines in the back yard and pinned with wooden clothespins. It was the weekly routine to put everything on the line to dry, and as soon as each child was old enough to help, we did. The result of drying laundry naturally in the low humidity and prevailing northwest wind was a pleasant, fresh scent that no modern method can duplicate.

On Saturday nights, the same kitchen area where the clothes were sorted became the place for our weekly baths. Using a square, galvanized steel tub about thirty-six inches on a side and sixteen inches high, we each took our bath. It was particularly cramped for those with long legs like Dad. Of course, babies were given more frequent baths, in a small tub in the kitchen sink. But after babyhood, the whole family in turn, beginning with the youngest who might still need assistance, and working up through our parents used the same bath water. Not to overdo, we washed our hair only every other week. Water was heated in tea kettles on the kitchen range and added as needed. Though there wasn't much privacy, it never seemed that anyone was spying on anyone. Luckily for me the bath practice changed just as I entered puberty.

We never had much money, but with the kitchen as the hub of our house we always had plenty to eat, clean clothes and a safe place for our many activities.

EIGHT

The Coming of the Refrigerator

It was a momentous day in 1948. Several years before electricity would come to our home, a truck arrived at our front door. Two men got out and laid a wooden ramp through our gate from the back of their truck to our front door. They wheeled in our new refrigerator. Anticipating the new appliance, Mom had shared her excitement with the children, "We will have ice cream in the refrigerator and ice for our Kool-Aid."

I was five, Gene was three, and Crysti, almost one. We boys were ready! As the off-white appliance with its rounded corners was coming through the door, Gene shouted, "Momma where is the ice cream? Can I have some?" He had not anticipated any delay. Gene's initial frustration at the wait for ice cream was short-lived, and we soon began to take refrigeration for granted.

There had been serious discussions leading to the purchase. I don't think Dad had ever experienced living with a refrigerator, but Mom had grown up in the small town of Timber Lake, where her father owned and operated a general store that surely had some refrigeration. When my parents felt they had the money, Dad did the research. Through a local store, Dad made a special order since refrigerators were not commonly in stock. (He probably bought it from the Farmers Union Co-op Oil

Company, where Dad was on the Board of Directors and served as its secretary for several years—although Mom was the one who carefully typed up the minutes for him.)

Our refrigerator was full-sized, though a little smaller than most we see today, and it had a small freezer compartment on top. The ammonia refrigerant was circulated by the heat of a burning cotton wick similar to those in our lamps. The flame was atop a squat steel kerosene tank located just above floor level, but below the refrigeration compartment. I have never seen another one like it. I was fascinated by the refrigerator, and as I got older, I thought about the process. How could a kerosene fire make the refrigerator cold? I still ponder that miracle.

We had to keep the fuel tank full, so the refrigerator was added to the list of things to fill every Saturday from our 65-gallon barrel of kerosene in the back yard. At first Dad did it, but when I was old enough Dad passed that job on to me.

Before the refrigerator came, we kept our milk and other perishable foods cool by lowering them in a bucket on a rope into an unused underground cistern near the house. The cistern was no longer suitable for water because it leaked. But the air in it was cooler in summer and often warmer in winter than the air at ground level. In retrospect that storage system seems frightfully crude and unsanitary, but it was what it was.

Twice a day Dad, and later Gene and I, milked our cow called Jersey. The raw milk was collected in an open stainless-steel bucket sterilized after each use. To remove flecks of dust and barnyard contaminants that might have blown into the milk, we poured it through a strainer with a paper filter and into #10 tin cans. We called the tins *gallon cans*, although they actually held only eleven cups, not sixteen.

After we had eaten the beans, peas, tomatoes, or peaches canned commercially, we re-purposed the cans for home storage. Each can had a ridge around its top and a seam running from top to bottom. The cans were always washed in hot soapy water and given a scalding rinse, but they surely were a haven for bacteria. We must have developed good immunity, since as far as I remember we never got sick from the raw milk stored in the cans. When we got the refrigerator, the cans were stored in it instead of the old cistern.

Frozen meat was kept in the commercial locker plant in Murdo, even after we got the refrigerator. Individual farm families rented cold storage lockers. Neighbors and family helped butcher each other's animals, and the owner of the locker plant cut, wrapped and froze the meat and stored it in the rented lockers. Our beef, pork or chicken was retrieved and brought home as needed. Before we had the refrigerator, frozen meat would be lowered into the old cistern where it stayed until it was to be used. The coming of the refrigerator, in spite of its small freezer compartment, certainly made that storage more convenient.

Even before the refrigerator came, we looked forward to a special frozen treat each winter. Dad ordered fish from a packing plant in Wisconsin. It came by train in a large cardboard box. Everything in the box was exotic to us: frozen mackerel, halibut, and many other kinds of fish common to most Americans nowadays. It was important to Dad that our family have the opportunity to appreciate seafood that was not readily available in our community. The order always came in the coldest part of the winter, and since it was in a box far too big to fit in the refrigerator, it was placed on sawhorses north of the house. In the shade, it remained frozen for weeks until we had time to consume all of the delicacies.

This seafood custom continued long after the arrival of the refrigerator, and we all enjoyed the yearly bounty of fish. At the time I did not fully appreciate the special effort on Dad's part to obtain it for us and on Mom's part to prepare so many things she was not familiar with. I still enjoy eating fish, now so readily available across the country.

The other winter experience, not affected by the arrival of the refrigerator, was making ice cream. We chipped ice off the dam and used it in our hand-cranked ice cream freezer with a little coarse salt on the ice to make the cranking easier. Our fresh whole milk was the major ingredient. Since Gene and I had winter birthdays, we always had fresh ice cream for our days. Wally's May birthday and Crysti's in July did not allow for that delicacy. I don't think that bags of ice were even available for purchase in stores in those days.

Having a refrigerator did not change other methods of preserving food. Vegetables and fruits were still home canned. Quart, pint, and jelly jars of cucumber or green bean pickles, stewed tomatoes, green and yellow beans, groundcherry jam and chokecherry jelly, and sometimes even sauerkraut were lined up neatly and colorfully on shelves in the cellar. Chicken and beef were also canned. I especially remember the flavor and texture of home-canned beef. After it had cooked a long time at high temperatures within the glass jars, either in a pressure cooker or in a big lightweight metal pot with a lid, called a *canner*, the grass-fed beef was more tender and juicier than that cooked in any other way. Mom often just heated up this beef and put it on the table as a main course, or she added it to a dish with macaroni or potatoes. I rarely taste any meat with the flavor and delicacy of the beef Mom canned.

The coming of the refrigerator was indeed a step forward for our family. It made life easier and safer, but its introduction did not alter the tradition of home canning and the wonderful dishes that came from it. Like the other farm wives and their small-town counterparts, Mom spent much of her summer canning food to be consumed in the winter. Although Mom tapered off her canning activities in her later years, her mother Crystal Bowder, living in Salem, Oregon had continued her prolific canning up to the year she died at the age of eighty-three.

NINE

Living Better with Electricity

Benjamin Franklin had experimented with electricity in the eighteenth century, Thomas Edison had invented electric lights and many other devices in the nineteenth century, and the 1893 Chicago World's Fair had established alternating current as the standard. But in the 1940s our home and neighboring farms in Jones County, South Dakota, were still lighted and heated by kerosene, stove oil, wood, or coal.

In 1945, Dad had installed a six-volt, direct current Wincharger mounted on a wooden tower with three large wet cell batteries in the cellar. Although it was an experiment that he, as a pacesetter and an innovator, felt compelled to do. I don't think this electricity changed our lives very much. It surely did not live up to Dad's expectations, and we didn't have lights like the towns. When there was no wind, we quickly depleted the charge in our batteries, the lights went out, and we were back on kerosene lamps. Really, *living* with electricity was still in the future.

Dad's introduction of the direct current wind generator to the community encouraged his father, Henry Roghair, who lived a few miles from us, to buy a much larger thirty-two-volt Wincharger that he mounted on a steel tower. It provided Grandpa and Grandma's home with power stored in sixteen batteries in their basement. Their system, of higher quality than ours, was, however, soon struck by lightning. Its batteries would no longer hold a charge, so my grandparents could only use their lights while the wind was blowing.

Grandpa was happy when he was able to hook up to a commercial 110/220 volt alternating current power line. It was called the Highline and ran along the highway connecting the small towns. The company did not consider it profitable to build lines to the scattered farms. But my grandparents lived close enough to the highway going through Okaton that the utility company wanted to place poles on their land. Grandpa negotiated a home connection as part of the easement agreement. Then they had power like the town.

In our house, beyond that six-volt system, the only electricity was from D cells in our flashlights and from the bigger batteries in the large AM radio and the crank telephone. On our farm, the car and truck ignitions used generators to produce their needed electricity while the tractor used a magneto.

At night our darkness was pristine. On clear nights, the stars shone brightly, and in winter we could often see the northern lights. From hilltops we could see dim dots of light produced by the kerosene lamps of the scattered farm homes. Driving up and down the hills on US 16, the highway that connected each small town along the Milwaukee Railroad, we could see distances of fifteen or more miles, often including the lights of one or more towns.

Many of the towns were large enough to have dazzling neon lights to advertise restaurants, hotels, bars, and other businesses. These lights were mesmerizing, so different from the lights we had in our home, and a glimpse into a world we were not a part of. Our sensation was akin to that expressed in the World War I song, "How ya gonna keep 'em down on the farm after they've seen Paree." Dad, through his incessant reading and curiosity, had glimpsed the other world and did not intend to live in the dark.

Before the Highline came, Okaton had had a gasoline powered generator that produced electricity for the town. I assume it may have been a thirty-two-volt DC system. (I don't remember seeing this system at work, but Gene and I discovered it in the weeds not far from the school.) When this system was replaced by the Highline, Okaton remained a small town—no one put up neon signs.

Dad's second utility venture was installing the telephone—the only one we had during the time we lived on the farm. The national Bell System was not available to rural homes until about 1960, but some of our neighbors put together a cooperative party line. The business model was quite simple: each homeowner took responsibility for putting up his own poles, stringing the single phone wire on glass insulators, and attaching the wire to the existing system. A crank phone in each home containing two large cylindrical dry cell batteries powered the system, and everyone was informed of a new home's chosen ring. The only joint expense was for materials to maintain the line running along the highway; the farmers did their own construction and maintenance work.

As a party line, every phone on the system would ring for every call made, regardless of whom it was for. And so, each home's ring had to be different—some combination of shorts and longs to be cranked by the caller. Ours was three longs. There was no privacy since anyone could listen in on any call. We were taught not to pick up other people's calls. But the rumor was that certain people were *rubbernecking* (as we called the eavesdropping) whenever the phone rang—although that could not be verified. None of our relatives, and only one other family from our church, were on this line. The participants were about ten farm families and the grocery store in Okaton that was operated by Mae Conger and her sister Ann Williams. They lived together in an apartment at the back of the store.

The crank phone in Conger's Store was on the wall beside the dial

Bell telephone—only one of two such phones in town; the other one was in the Okaton State Bank. A single jack could connect our party line to the Bell world. Since the store was also the Post Office for some years, Mae Conger was not only postmistress but telephone operator on the rare occasion that a long-distance call came in for someone on the party line. The patched connection wasn't always good. I remember our family receiving a call from relatives in Oregon, but then getting in the car and driving the three and a half miles into Okaton because the party line connection was too poor. Yet without having our own phone, we would not have even known that someone in Oregon wanted to talk to us.

Dad's largest utility venture was to become part of the local support for the project of the national Rural Electrical Administration (REA), which had begun to make rural power a possibility in 1935. The work in our area only began in earnest about 1950. Dad, always interested in cooperatives, became an advocate. I remember accompanying him when he visited neighbors to encourage them to join the co-op that would put up the lines and manage the power to be purchased from a coal powered generating plant in the Black Hills. The advocacy he participated in was successful, and the West Central Electric Cooperative, Inc. was formed with its headquarters in Murdo.

When we did get our first on-the-grid power in 1952, we were ready for it. Before all the tall wooden poles, dipped in pungent black creosote, were in place, and before the cables bringing the electricity were connected, Dad had wired our home. Even though he had not been allowed to go to high school, and with two winter courses in diesel mechanics constituting his only higher education, he was always studying. He purchased technical books and taught himself electrical wiring, so he was able to wire our house. I don't know if there were any enforceable codes in the rural area, but Dad took no risks and hired a licensed electrician to come inspect his work before the power came on. What Dad had done passed inspection and our house was ready.

Months ahead of the arrival of REA power, we had begun to live with electricity. Dad had purchased and installed in the garage a 110-volt alternating current generator powered by a one-cylinder, two-cycle Briggs and Stratton gasoline engine. It was a little larger than similar engines we used to power a grain auger and an irrigation pump for the vegetable garden. Such engines were started by a vigorous pull on a cotton rope wound around the pulley attached to the flywheel. The generator not only gave us a few weeks' jump on our neighbors who had to wait for the REA power, but it was a back-up source—especially welcome in the early months, when frequent power outages would last hours at a time.

Mom was having a difficult pregnancy with our youngest brother, Wallace, in the spring of 1952. So, before the REA power arrived, any respite from housework was welcome for her. Dad purchased an Ironrite, a small electric mangle. Seated in front of this machine with its fabric-covered roller and hot metal press, Mom experienced a transformation of her weekly job of ironing clothes that had required so much standing. She was more than ready to give up the iron that was fueled by white gasoline, had to be pumped up like a camp stove, and lit with a match. She was also happy to let the older cast iron ones, solid and heavy, become door stops. No longer would they be heated in the oven with the risk of skin burns as their wooden handles were clipped on. Gene and I, seven and nine, had already learned to help with the ironing and were now eager to operate the Ironrite. Our lives had changed forever.

Gene, a curious young man, got permission to take the old gas iron apart to see how it worked. Dad agreed to let him study it, provided he would put it back together, which he promised to do. But as the years went by, it was never reassembled, and I don't think anyone really missed it. We had electricity.

TEN

Living in the Whole House

We spent much of our time at home outdoors. The room in our house where the most activities happened was our kitchen. But I have vivid memories to share of the rest of the house, as well.

Isolated as we were, it was always exciting when visitors came into our driveway. They came to our front door that opened to a small hallway. Straight ahead was another door to the stairs and the second floor. I never went upstairs when I was small; perhaps it had been locked. Visitors certainly didn't go there either, nor would they go into our parents' bedroom to the right. Instead, they would turn left into the small living room where the wallpaper was a soft shade of gray with a little red design. A wood/coal-burning Warm Morning Stove of sturdy steel and imported from Mexico stood in one corner. It was attached to the central chimney along with the kitchen range on the other side of the wall. Together they were the heat source for the entire house.

The battery-powered AM tube radio, in its bulky wooden case, sat on a shelf across from the stove. It was our only connection to the outside world, so it was important to have new batteries on hand when they were needed. Dad ordered the large round dry cells from Sears Roebuck or Montgomery Ward.

We didn't have many books on the shelves below the radio, but some that we did have were well-used, especially the Bible and children's Bible story books. I was personally drawn to the anatomical drawings in a home medical book. Three special books Mom had kept from her college days were *The Merriam Webster Collegiate Dictionary, The Complete Works of Shakespeare,* and a book of world literature for children containing Greek, Roman, and Norse tales. There were a few assorted other titles. The shelf was close enough to the kitchen table that we could always retrieve the dictionary when needed for a discussion during a meal.

The living room had a couch, the kind that could fold out into a bed for visitors, albeit a rather uncomfortable one. There was a stuffed swivel chair that we could spin around and around, although we were not supposed to. In the middle of the room was just enough space to set up a card table and folding chairs—an alternative to playing games on the kitchen table. One game we could only play in the living room was Caroms. For that game we used a square board with pockets in the corners to catch wooden rings as they were propelled by wooden sticks—a game a little like pool.

The living room was small and modestly comfortable for visitors, but the time sitting there with company was often shortened by a move to the kitchen table for coffee or milk and cake or cookies. Like the rest of the house this room changed over the years. The Warm Morning Stove was replaced by the floor furnace that hung into the cellar. The furnace was placed in a hole sawed into the floor of the doorway between the living room and the kitchen, so in place of that section of the floor was a metal grate we could stand over to warm up on winter days. The furnace burned stove oil, about the same grade of petroleum as kerosene. The fuel was stored in an above-ground tank just north of the house and piped by gravity to the furnace hanging from the ceiling of the cellar.

One extremely cold night, after we had all gone to bed, Dad heard the furnace click off. He realized immediately that the stove oil in the pipe had frozen. He got out of bed, dressed, located the flashlight and blowtorch, and went out to heat the pipe. He got the oil flowing again, and we did not freeze. Thawing the pipe was a nasty job that night, but overall, the furnace took less work than the Warm Morning Stove it had replaced that had to be fed daily.

Dad was always interested in both healthy eating and home remedies. After the furnace was installed, he prepared a concoction of benzoin, eucalyptus oil and water in a tin can and placed it on the upper surface of the combustion chamber of the furnace, just below floor level. The evaporating oils gave our home a special, pleasing fragrance in the cold season. With these vapors, Vicks VapoRub and Vaseline for our noses, and a spoonful of cod liver oil before we went to bed each night, we did well fending off colds and flu.

The party line telephone took its place on the wall near where the Warm Moring Stove had been. It was easily answered anytime it rang three longs since it was centrally located, only a few steps from the kitchen table or the range.

The four first-floor rooms, that comprised our home's entire living space when I was small, were all connected. Each room of the rectangular house had a door or entryway into the rooms on either side. They formed a circular path for children to run around and around. Of course, that was not permitted, but it was always a tempting possibility especially on a rainy day or during a blizzard. Running or not, we fully occupied the first floor.

When Gene and I were small, we had bunk beds in the smallest room. One door of our room was to the kitchen and the other to our parents' room. Because I was older, I slept on the top bunk, and Gene, on the bottom. One night I fell from the top bunk onto the floor and didn't even wake up. Dad picked me up and found me uninjured. I must have been a heavy sleeper.

Beside the bed we always had a red-trimmed white enamel pot with a lid. It was only to be used during the night and was, without fail, to be dumped in the outdoor toilet the next morning by the one who used it. If we did forget, a disaster could strike as two little boys romped around the room. If dumping was delayed longer, and there was no spill, we had the smell to contend with. We tried our best not to forget.

Each night, as Mom or sometimes Dad put us to bed, we heard a story. It may have been one from Mom's big children's literature book or from one of a few smaller children's books. Then we knelt beside the lower bunk and said the evening prayer that many children have:

Now I lay me down to sleep.
I pray the Lord my soul to keep.
If I should die before I wake,
I pray the Lord my soul to take.

I don't think we ever thought about how foreboding those final words were. We cheerfully continued by asking God to bless Mama, Daddy, and all our siblings, grandparents and sometimes a list of aunts and uncles and cousins by name. We concluded with, "Amen."

When I was going to sleep on the top bunk, with only the wooden door between our bedroom and that of our parents, I remember sometimes hearing the sound of squeaking bed springs. I was not disturbed by the sounds and do not remember ever invading their privacy in the night.

Mom and Dad's room, between our bedroom and the front hallway, was not large. Besides their simple double bed there was Mom's vanity with a big round mirror. Mom and Dad shared a high dresser with drawers, and a small closet for hanging clothes. In this room they slept at night and sometimes took an hour or two of rest on a Sunday afternoon. I remember rising early a few mornings to see them kneeling together beside their bed, praying before the start of their day.

Mom and Dad's bed was also where we children would spend the day if we were too sick to go to school. If our stomachs were upset a pail was set beside the bed in case we had to throw up. We got a dose of liquid Pepto-Bismol, but I always felt that made me sicker. In order not to waste the day by being sick, Mom would bring out a set of small, cheap, but elegant-looking hardback books published in 1898 but given to her in 1937. They were by Henry Wadsworth Longfellow: *The Song of Hiawatha*, *The Courtship of Miles Standish*, *Evangeline*, and *Tales of a Wayside Inn*. I was never sick long enough to get through any of those books, but I do remember them as a part of my recovery process.

As we grew older and there were more of us, we began to use the second floor. Crystal was born the summer I was four. Gene and I were still using the bunkbeds in the tiny bedroom. Crysti, as we always called her, spent her first few months sleeping in a crib in our parents' room. During that time, she came down with the whooping cough before she was old enough to be vaccinated. Our parents did not talk to us about the danger she was in, but I did sense the gravity of the situation. Thankfully, she lived through the trauma and became a healthy child.

The next year, Crysti's crib was moved into our small room, and we boys moved to the second floor. Our new room had roof-sloped side walls, a south-facing window at one end, and the stairs coming up at the other. It seemed to us a grand space. A small kerosene lamp sat on the dresser beside our bed. I was assigned to light it every night using a wooden match, and to fill it with fuel every Saturday. One of our parents would blow out the lamp after coming up to say good night, or I could do it if we had all had goodnight kisses before we went up to bed. Gene was soon old enough to light the lamp himself. Gene and I shared an old double bed and two dressers. A bookshelf beside the stairs was placed as a guardrail to keep us safe in the dark or during daytime rough play.

It was Mom's rule that we spend time every Saturday morning cleaning our huge new space. I always labored over where to put things away properly and thus made hard work of straightening up. But, as I remember it, Gene considered it sufficient to pile everything into the storage space opening into our room and under the eaves beside the walls of the smaller room. Closing the plywood door finished the project, and he was done cleaning. I never felt that efficient. We usually got along well but did not always see things the same way.

Wally was born when I was nine, and a little later Crysti moved to the smaller room upstairs with the north-facing window. With one of the bunkbeds becoming a single, she had a private bedroom—all to herself. The door to her room was at the top of the stairs in our room.

Wally spent his first year or so sleeping in the crib in our parents' bedroom and then in the tiny room on the first floor where Gene and I had had our bunk beds. But by that time other things were moving into that space. Electricity came to our house about the time Wally was born. When Mom got the Ironrite mangle it needed a home, so it was placed in the small room that Wally would soon have. When it was time for him to have more space, he joined us in the boys' bedroom on the upper floor. The second of the bunk beds came with him, so among the three boys we had a double bed and a single.

Before long, an electric power-spin washing machine joined the Ironrite in the small room. It replaced the Maytag wringer machine with the gasoline motor on the back porch. Things were moving quickly, and soon Dad cut a door to the porch into the wall, about where our bunk beds had originally been. He walled off the north end of the porch to become an indoor bathroom. An electric pump in the cellar droned every time we ran any water. The noise of the pump could be heard all over the house, a warning not to waste the water that was still coming into our cistern by truck. We had a flush toilet, but it was not for us to use often. We did have the luxury of a real private bathtub; that I particularly appreciated. But we still saved and shared our bathwater.

As the bathroom was added, Dad had a well-driller dig a circular hole to be our new cesspool in place of the one he had earlier dug by hand. To benefit the cottonwood tree that had thrived so well on the weekly laundry water, he placed the new cesspool near it. But the unexpected consequence was that the tree, that had been so blessed by weekly water, was shocked. Its roots had remained near the surface because that is where it had found the weekly wash water. Suddenly all the water draining from the house and any rainwater falling in the vicinity soaked down several yards deeper than the roots of the tree. The tree died within a year. (It was a lesson on the value of deep roots that crept into more than one sermon in my adult career.)

During the fifteen years my parents lived in their little house with their growing family, they succeeded in improving it, making the most of every inch of its space, and creating our "home on the range."

A well-worn picture of our home taken in early 1940s
from west of the house with dam in foreground.

The front of our house, from the east in early morning (note shadow).

Gene and Jim on sawhorses in back yard near trash burner. Old shed on left, barn on right.

Jim on Boots, Gene standing.

Enjoying an early snow. Thanksgiving weekend in mid 1950s. All four Roghair children and weekend guests on sled and toboggan.

PART C

How I Learned

ELEVEN

Born into Okaton Reformed Church

I was born into the Okaton Church. It was a part of the fabric of our family's life from the time it was organized in 1925. My grandparents Henry and Cornelia Roghair became two of its founding members shortly after they moved to the community from northwest Iowa. This church was part of my life, from my birth and baptism in 1943 until we moved away in 1957 when I was starting high school. Ours was a small congregation of the Reformed Church in America, often called the Dutch Reformed because of it direct relationship to the state Reformed Church in the Netherlands.

Every Sunday our extended family joined with other families not only for a time of worship and religious education, but also a time of socializing. As mostly farm families, we shared common interests. The Sunday attendance numbered between thirty and fifty. Despite its short history, when I was born, the congregation had already become an institution with its own customs and expectations—spoken and unspoken.

The decision-making and control of the congregation were family-related, involving loyalties, squabbles, and rivalries. There were the predictable small church lead elders through whom most decisions were processed—my Roghair grandparents in this church. We were a small enough group that we knew whom to expect every week, and we always noted when someone was missing. When visitors came, everyone was eager to meet them and learn what their connections might be. The church was a tight-knit group, and we didn't strive to increase its membership. So, it was a surprise if someone local visited unexpectedly. We were a family church in every sense of that phrase; normally one was either born or married into it. But for some it seemed difficult to be absorbed into the texture of the congregation even by marriage. Our mother was the first non-Dutch spouse in Dad's immediate family—although her grandpa Swearingen certainly carried a Dutch family name. But I think that Mom always felt herself a bit of an outsider to the Roghair family and our church.

When I was growing up, the church membership was mostly two large multigenerational farm families, the Roghairs and the Daums. The Oldenkamps from Murdo included three children about my age, but as they had more children, they became a large delegation. Their father worked on state road maintenance. There were a few other small families and individuals.

We knew which row of slatted wooden chairs each family would occupy. There were six or eight rows with five or six chairs on either side of the center aisle. My parents chose our family's place in the last row on the left, closest to the large oil-burning stove that heated the room in winter. My grandparents sat a row or two forward, and my cousins sat across the aisle.

I especially liked to sit near the window. Long before my time, the clear glass windows had been covered with a decorative film to give the appearance of stained glass. The covering was deteriorating, and the film was peeling off. When I sat by the window, I could sneak my hand up and scratch off a little of it. If my mother saw that, she scolded me with a scowl or a reprimand under her breath. But I needed a diversion to get through the long services. I often sucked the coins I had been given to put in the offering plate. They always had a salty taste. As I think about it now, all these years later, the idea of putting coins in my mouth is offensive and hard to imagine, not to mention unhygienic. I doubt my parents saw me do it.

Once in a while, I could sit on Grandpa Roghair's left side while Grandma sat on his right. Of course, there were at least eight other grandkids there every Sunday, so it was an opportunity we shared. Although sitting by Grandpa meant keeping really still—something I never found easy—there was always a reward. In his pocket he always found two round pink mint candies. He would put one in his mouth and give the other to the grandchild sitting next to him.

We began to get ready for church on Saturday night. We always had "dress-up shoes" for Sunday. They were never badly scuffed, like our everyday shoes, since we never wore them in the barnyard, for any work, or to school. But Mom made sure we polished our shoes every week. We applied paste wax (never the liquid kind) with a small brush or rag and a little water. The shoes were shined as well as possible with a flat, wooden-handled cotton buffer.

In the morning, we dressed in our Sunday best. Perceptions of appropriate dress were deeply held. Mothers and daughters wore dresses or skirts and blouses; for the men and boys a suit was in order, although the "suit" was usually slacks and a sport coat accompanied by a tie. Boys may not have always had a sport jacket or tie, but at least no one ever wore blue jeans or overalls to church—that would never do.

Bob, my youngest uncle, told a story of how his mother Cornelia came to the aid of a family during the depression of the 1930s. The adult son of a couple in the church had died. The mother and father were desperate; if they buried their son appropriately dressed in a suit, what would the father wear to the funeral? Perhaps a pattern had not been noticed or had been politely ignored by fellow church members; the father and son had been alternating their church attendance because they only had one suit between them. By coming on alternating Sundays, they had managed to stay within the accepted dress code, and the family's pride remained intact.

In the midst of their mourning, the approaching funeral brought a crisis to the parents that Grandma was able to solve. She made over an old suit of Grandpa's for the corpse to wear. The father could then be appropriately attired for the funeral. As I was growing up in the 1940s and 1950s, I do not remember any such desperation, but the underlying dress code has always seemed quite familiar to me.

Of course, dressing properly was not our only weekly ritual. On Sundays, we were never allowed to go fishing or to play outdoor games. The only farm work we could do was to feed the animals, make sure they had water, and milk the cow. Sometimes we would go as a family to visit relatives or friends. But on Sunday afternoons when we were home and going nowhere, Mom reminded us to start reading our Sunday School lesson for the next week. We always received a one-sheet Sunday School paper with a printed lesson. I remember the junior paper best. It was folded into four pages. A short passage from the King James Version of the Bible—about one chapter—was in the first column. An explanatory article followed with discussion questions, and other articles of interest to our age group were included. We were expected to read the paper before next Sunday's class. If we hadn't finished it on the previous Sunday afternoon, it was an unquestioned expectation to do so on Saturday night along with the shoe-shining.

I liked Sunday School more than church, as we called the worship service. Adults and children, thirty or more of us, divided up into four or five classes—usually pre-school, primary, intermediate, young people, and adults. We met in various locations in the structure's single room.

My preschool Sunday School teacher was Miss Lampert. She had grown up in Phillip located on the North Western Railroad in the next county, but not far from Okaton. She came to fulfill the role of

Superintendent of the Okaton School. She brought impressive credentials including a master's degree in education. When she arrived, we had no idea that she would marry Uncle Albert Roghair and become our Aunt Eva. She was always kind and attentive when she talked with little kids, whether as their teacher or informally.

When I was in the primary class our teacher was Elizabeth Daum, the widowed mother of the other large family in the church. She used a flannel board on which she placed cutouts of Biblical characters with fabric on the back to hold them to the board. They could be moved and replaced to show action—an early version of audiovisuals. Later, Aunt Grace Roghair, mother of all my local cousins, taught that group. Grace always gave gifts to her class. I remember a tiny book she gave me with a few verses from each book of the Bible. One Sunday Grandpa came to the primary class and told me it was time for me to join the intermediate class he was teaching. My older cousins Richard and Lawrence were already in that group.

Music was always an important part of our church—vigorous congregational singing accompanied by the piano. There was never a choir. In both Sunday School and worship, we always sang with gusto. I particularly remember the piano-playing of Aunt Joanna Roghair and later my cousins Richard and Lorraine Roghair. A cousin of the Daum family came to stay with them for several summers, and while he was there, he often played piano for our church. Dad commented on how much he appreciated the way the young man played strong bass notes. But even hearing the prominent bass, Dad could not find the notes with his voice. No matter how much he loved to sing, he was never able to carry a tune or any harmony part. Yet he made a joyful noise and was not shy in belting out the words. Some people claimed they loved to hear him sing—even though he was always off pitch.

Grandpa Roghair, with his especially strong baritone, sang the melody, so his was always the dominant voice. In my primary grade school years, Grandpa was the Sunday School Superintendent, which meant he led a time of singing for the whole group before we divided into our separate classes. Each week he picked a hymn or two and then let others make requests. The songbooks we were using had mostly hymns and gospel songs from the late nineteenth and early twentieth century with a few older hymns. For some inexplicable reason, a Southern gospel song by a Baptist composer had caught Grandpa's fancy. It seems we sang it every week: "Life's Railway to Heaven."

> *Life is like a mountain railroad,*
> > *With an engineer that's brave;*
> *We must make the run successful,*
> > *From the cradle to the grave;*
> *Watch the curves, the fills, the tunnels;*
> > *Never falter, never quail;*
> *Keep your hand upon the throttle,*
> > *And your eye upon the rail.* (Text, M. E. Abbey; tune,
> Charlie Tillman)

At home Mom irreverently remarked that the church had to get new books that didn't contain that song. I don't know that Mom had any part in picking the new books we eventually got, but they did not contain the song. Even so, we had sung it so often, that it still resonates in my ears. The song was recorded by Johnny Cash and by many other country and gospel artists. It is a mystery why it should have become such a favorite for the farmer who had never worked on the railroad and who lived over one hundred miles from a mountain. But poetry and song do transcend time and space.

I wasn't consciously trying to mimic Grandpa's obsession with a single song, but, when I was in first grade, I began to quickly raise my hand every Sunday to request my special one, "The Church in the Wildwood":

There's a church in the valley by the wildwood,
    No lovelier spot in the dale;
No place is so dear to my childhood
    As the little brown church in the vale.

The tenors and basses begin the refrain singing:

Oh, come, come, come, come. . .

and continue to sing *come* a total of nineteen times while the altos and sopranos sing above their *coming*:

Come to the church in the wildwood,
    Oh, come to the church in the vale.

All complete the refrain:

No spot is so dear to my childhood
    As the little brown church in the vale. (Text and tune, William S. Pitts)

Like Grandpa, I was indifferent to the fact that others might get tired of singing the same song so often—especially with its interminable repetitions. Within its four verses and refrains the word *come* appears a total of eighty-six times. My choice was as removed from our daily lives as was Grandpa's. The actual Little Brown Church was in Iowa, and our own little white church was no closer to any wild woods than it was to a mountain railroad.

Occasionally someone would plan a piece of special music for the service. It was always welcomed by the congregation and added to the order of worship by whatever minister was leading that day. Mom sometimes prepared me to do special music. One Easter morning I accompanied myself on the Hawaiian (steel) guitar I was learning to play, and I sang "Christ Arose." It begins solemnly:

Low in the grave He lay Jesus my Savior. . .

and has an upbeat refrain:

Up from the grave he arose,
    With a mighty triumph o'er his foes;
He arose a Victor from the dark domain,
    And He lives forever with His saints to reign,
He arose! He arose! Hallelujah! Christ arose! (Text and tune, Robert Lowery.)

Several years later, when my voice was beginning to change, Mom taught me the alto, and she sang the melody to an 1874 hymn written by Mary Ann Baker, "Master, the Tempest Is Raging." Joining her in that duet one Sunday morning was my first experience of part-singing.

Our services were informal, with no printed bulletin. Sometimes a visiting minister would be surprised as the service progressed. How was he to know that on the third hymn the people would remain seated, and the elected deacon would pass the offering plate? The members expected it—that's the way we did it every week. Our small church had its own practices and internal leadership. It didn't expect much from the clergy beyond preaching a sermon and offering prayers. Officiating at baptisms, communions, funerals, and weddings, were infrequent but limited to ministers ordained in the Reformed Church of America, all of whom lived at some distance from our community. The life of the church moved along with consistency even as clergy came and went.

TWELVE

The Life of the Okaton Reformed Church

To the best of my knowledge, I was baptized as an infant by Rev. B. D. Dykstra. He was sixty-one, and it was late in his career by that time. Rev. Dykstra seems to have preferred going by his initials over his full name Broe Doekeles, as he had been christened in Friesland, the Netherlands. Rev. Dykstra was a revered and legendary figure in our congregation. Okaton Reformed Church had been founded in June 1925, and he was undoubtedly instrumental in facilitating that process. His obituary indicates that from 1924 to 1931 he was the Classical Missionary for the Dakotas. (In the Dutch and German Reformed denominations, *classical* refers to the classis which is a regional denominational governing body composed of equal numbers of clergy and elected congregational elders. These denominations share a presbyterian ecclesiastical structure, so the classis is comparable to the presbytery in Scottish churches and their descendant denominations.)

As missionary to the recently settled two-state Dakota population, Rev. Dykstra worked in communities having significant Dutch settlements assisting them to organize their churches. No wonder he was

79

highly regarded by our congregation. During the Okaton Church's early years, a Reformed minister, although not always Rev. Dykstra, came to Okaton once a month to conduct services. For the other Sundays, local arrangements had to be made. I do not know who would have been available to lead, perhaps a local Methodist minister, or maybe one of the members of our church—like my grandfather.

When I was a boy, I was unaware of Rev. Dykstra's occupational credentials, but I remember his being referred to as "the minister on a bicycle." That he was—one internet biography estimates that he rode more than 20,000 miles in his lifetime. He and his bike must have come to Okaton by train since it would have been exhausting to navigate by bicycle the original US 16 or any pathway available before it was built. Besides that, ministers could ride the train for free. But when he got to Okaton, Rev. Dykstra surely travelled the dirt roads locally on his bike—visiting people and selling religious books he had written.

In his lifetime, Rev. Dykstra held various career positions. As an educator, he was teacher, superintendent, and principal of church-related and public schools in South Dakota. As church leader, he served in classical roles and pastored churches in South Dakota and Iowa. He was an author and publisher of religious books in both Dutch and English and became the editor of *Volksvried*, a Dutch-language newspaper published in Orange City, Iowa, that my dad liked to read in the 1950s. Rev. Dykstra is remembered as a pacifist.

With my dad, I visited Rev. Dykstra once in his later years. I don't remember whether it was in Orange City, Iowa, or somewhere in eastern South Dakota. If I had known him better, he might have been a role model for me.

There was never a large enough membership to afford a full-time resident pastor in Okaton, so the congregation experienced a variety of preachers over the years. The first one I remember, when I was about five, was a Reformed minister, Rev. Henry Nyhof. For a year or two he added an afternoon worship for our church to his Sunday schedule after leading morning worship near his home in Lakeview, South Dakota. It became a grueling schedule especially in the winter—weekly trips of driving about seventy miles each way, mostly on US 83, a gravel road at the time. But during summer months he even stayed late in Okaton to do Sunday evening services.

Once, when I was with Dad in Lakeview for some reason, we stopped to visit Rev. Nyhof. Dad learned that not only was he serving the two churches so many miles apart, he was also farming to make ends meet. I was too young to fully understand the details, but I remember Dad then attempting to find a way to increase Rev. Nyhof's compensation.

After the relationship with Rev. Nyhof ended, there was a short-term arrangement with Rev. Cronin, the Methodist pastor already serving the Methodist congregations in Murdo and Draper, the two towns to our east. Then there was Rev. Terry, a Presbyterian pastor of two and sometimes three Presbyterian churches in Kadoka, Belvidere and Phillip, towns west and northwest of us. Those must have been long Sundays for him.

For several summers we had the privilege of assigned student pastors from Western Theological Seminary in Holland, Michigan. They stayed with one of the church families, often my grandparents. It was refreshing to meet these students and experience their leadership in morning and evening services for the whole summer.

In the late 1950s, Rev. Marcus Moget, a retired Reformed minister from the Netherlands, moved to Okaton with his wife and served as pastor for a few years. The Netherlands' reputation was as a place where Protestants, Catholics, and Jews lived harmoniously, but my experience of this pastor challenged that view. It must have been an attitude he brought from Europe that prompted him to preach anti-Catholic sermons. I had never heard that kind of preaching before. He also seemed to hold antipathy toward other Protestant denominations. Dad recalled that Rev. Moget had commiserated with Grandpa that his son was planning to marry a Baptist, but Grandpa reprimanded him saying, "You should be glad he is marrying a Christian."

Perhaps the comfortable interaction among denominations in small-town America was new to Rev. Moget. There was a tiny Roman Catholic church in town, and we were friends with its members. Our own church had experienced interdenominational relationships from its beginning. Its original place of worship was a one-room building that had been constructed by community volunteers with some resources from the Methodist Episcopal Church (the official name at the time). The property title was then held by the Methodist Conference, and the two congregations cooperated to schedule their services at different hours to avoid conflicts. A joint Sunday School met weekly between the services when that schedule worked. Perhaps the cooperative nature of the Sunday School had been more evident in the earlier years, because by the time I was involved, the Sunday School seemed to belong to our church alone.

Usually, our congregation's winter services were in the afternoon to accommodate the need for farm families to provide hay and water for cattle in the morning. In summer, services were usually Sunday mornings, with additional less formal ones in the evening. The youth group met Sunday evenings after the services, or in place of them during the winter. I was too young to be involved in the youth group until the summer I graduated from eighth grade. So, I had only a taste of that experience before we moved away.

By the mid-1950s the Okaton Methodist Church was dwindling, and the Reformed congregation was feeling the need for more space. Our church leaders requested of the Methodist Conference a fifty-year lease on the building we shared and permission to dig a basement under it. When the request was denied, our congregation of mostly farmers proceeded to build its own house of worship on a small plot of unbroken prairie provided by a friend of the church. It was a half mile off the townsite and near the new Highway 16—even closer to today's I-90. A sad footnote to this story is that the Methodist Church was closed within a few years. Its building was sold and perhaps moved to a nearby farm to become a garage, and the lot has been vacant ever since.

Under the supervision of my uncle Jack Roghair, the men of the church and community, with the support of women and children, worked long and hard to build a new structure. Every detail of the construction was accomplished by volunteers—the design, the carpentry, and even the crafting of the pulpit and communion table. Only the wiring was contracted to a licensed electrician. Later, when Dad had successfully wired our own home, and it passed the inspection of a licensed electrician, we realized that he surely could have properly wired the church—even without a license.

Our new church had a basement that could accommodate several Sunday School classes and serve as a social gathering space. Originally, no kitchen was built. Grandma Roghair had grown up in the more conservative Christian Reformed Church (also Dutch), and she was adamantly opposed to having a kitchen in the church. Since no water was required in the new building, and there would be nearby outhouses that everyone was familiar with, there was no need for a cistern.

Nonetheless, after Grandma was gone, a simple kitchen was added. When water began to be piped to the region from the Oahe Dam, indoor plumbing became commonplace. The church stands today, changed very little from when it was built—plain glass windows, no steeple or bell—a simple place of worship—although its denominational affiliation has changed.

Besides worship and study, our church was also a place of social gathering. Various age and gender groupings found each other on Sundays, before, after, and between Sunday School and worship. I particularly remember standing in the dirt parking area along with my three older male cousins, our two youngest uncles, and others about our age, while we bragged about (or at least compared) how many rattlesnakes we had each killed so far that summer. It was always a matter of us against the snakes, and we weren't burdened by any concern for preserving their species. After cutting off a rattlesnake head with a garden hoe, a spade, or whatever one had at hand, the custom was to step on the snake's body and pull off the rattles—a sort of trophy. We understood that a new segment of rattle had been added each time the snake had shed its skin—one or more times per summer. The longer the snake and the larger the rattles, the more prestige for the one telling his story. I don't remember it being necessary to bring the rattles to church to verify our claims.

But our camaraderie wasn't all about snakes. We could also compare how much rain we had gotten—everybody had a rain gauge—or how high the snow drifts were in the winter. There was never widespread uniformity during any particular weather event. In season, we might discuss how many acres of summer fallow we had worked, or the older ones might tease the younger about the rows of weeds left in the summer fallow from not having driven the tractor carefully enough. During harvest, it was always appropriate to discuss how many bushels per acre various fields produced, or how much hay we had hauled. The possibilities for farm trivia were endless. If there was nothing else to discuss, the virtues of various brands of tractors or vehicles might be debated. Families had great loyalties, so if someone was having trouble with a Chevrolet, he might be sarcastically encouraged to jack up the radiator cap and drive a Ford under it. The boys and young men had their rousing discussions, but certainly the girls, adult women, and older men had their own discussions as they huddled in their separate groups.

In my preteen and early teen years, I enjoyed going to the summer Sunday evening services with my dad while the rest of the family stayed home. These services, led by our summer student pastor, when we had one, or by Rev. Moget, after he came, were more relaxed than those earlier in the day. There was more singing, and the sermons seemed more engaging. Perhaps they were less theological and more practical than in the morning.

Celebrations during the church year were few. We didn't pay attention to a liturgical calendar beyond Easter and Christmas. Of course, Easter was observed, but without much added decoration or deviation in the order of service to distinguish it from other Sundays. Things went along without much variation Sunday by Sunday. The Christmas Eve program was a large event beyond the weekly routine. Several families who did not attend regularly made sure their children got to Sunday School to practice for and be a part of that yearly program. The other big celebration was of a national holiday. The Sunday School Fourth of July picnic was held in someone's hay field or cow pasture.

Daily Vacation Bible School was held for a week or two in the Summer—a shared experience for the children and some adult volunteers—usually held in the Okaton School building. We studied a biblical curriculum designed for our various age groups, learned music to sing for our parents on the final night, and always did a handicraft project. A farm couple, Johnny Weaver, my Aunt Grace's brother, and his wife Henrietta had mastered leathercraft. They made tooled belts, purses, and other assorted items. It was exciting to learn the craft from them. I used that knowledge to make things I exhibited on 4-H Rally Days and for a project that fulfilled a county handicraft requirement for eighth grade graduation.

Even though our congregation was small and had no wealthy benefactors, it had a good reputation for giving to missions. Often missionaries on home leave made their way across the prairie to stop at our little church for a weeknight presentation to interpret their work and solicit our support. Of all the church's weekly or yearly activities, the missionary visits were the most inspiring to me personally. Their slide presentations carried me into worlds that I knew in no other way, since television had not yet entered our lives.

Among those who came were visitors from the Cameroons, China, Japan, and somewhere in the Muslim Middle East. I still remember some Chinese words a missionary taught me when I was in first or second grade. Pictures of people in Africa—sometimes women wearing no tops—seemed to need someone to teach them to be more proper. I have probably forgotten some of the locations our visitors were serving. Dad regularly communicated with a missionary in the Philippines. He also received newsletters from R.G. LeTourneau, the successful inventor and manufacturer of earthmoving machinery, who then initiated missionary, social, and business involvements in Peru. His newsletters shared his work and ideas. Both his machines and his mission work were inspiring to Dad.

When I was about twelve years old, I heard a presentation by a missionary couple serving in Japan. I don't remember the specifics of their personalities, how they spoke, or what they said. Their message and presentation were similar to others I had been hearing as long as I could remember. But something clicked within me—it was what people often describe as a *call from God*.

I had been thinking and praying about my life for the past two years after my fourth-grade teacher had called me out at school to act like a big boy. About the same time, I had raised my hand and gone forward at a revival service in the Methodist Church in Murdo as an act of accepting Jesus. It was a malleable period in my life. I was looking for appropriate ways to take my place in the world. So, when I heard the missionaries from Japan, I was receptive, and I began to wonder: was I being called to be a missionary?

Overseas and domestic missionary activity—reaching out to non-Christians—was a significant part of the Protestant milieu of the time. Congregations gave money, paying for services performed at distant places by their representatives. The support of this type of missionary activity has sometimes been compared to the way military campaigns are staged. Our little church was definitely a part of this larger system, and it was a part of what I knew growing up.

I was proud to be the son of a farmer and enjoyed our life on the farm. I was at the age of beginning to take a larger role in the work of the farm, and only two years younger than the age at which my father began to farm for himself. I looked forward to becoming a farmer, too, and I expected that I might take on leadership in the church and community that I had seen my grandpa and my dad take on. Although I felt comfortable in those expectations, the religious call was shaking that certainty.

I began to think and pray about my options. I wrestled privately for several weeks or months and did not discuss this dilemma with anyone else. Finally, it became clear to me that I was being called to pursue a life of Christian service. When I finally told my parents I was going to be a missionary, they seemed pleased, and it soon became known and accepted in our Church.

It was ironic that I had arrived at this decision several years before I was even allowed to be confirmed as a member of the church. I had asked Dad if I could join the church, but he said I couldn't do it until my cousin Richard did, and he was two years older. So I waited, even while adult church members expressed their affirmation that I would be a missionary.

My church membership wasn't actually completed until I started high school in Oregon, and my parents joined the Presbyterian Church in McMinnville. There I found that all the teens my age had taken a confirmation class and were already members. So, I did not join in the customary way with membership class—I just had a meeting or two with the pastor, and I joined alone one Sunday. But my call to ministry remained clear.

In my ordained career I never became a missionary to Africa or Asia. Instead, I was called to work in African American communities of poverty in rural Georgia and inner-city Cincinnati, Newark, and Chicago. I spent many years in the rural Iñupiaq communities of Arctic Alaska, as well as short periods in mostly White congregations of several denominations. During the first two and a half decades of ministry I shared life and ministry with my wife Willa, whom I had met in seminary. She and I became a part of an early wave of clergy couples in the 1970s. We brought two sons into the world who were then dubbed *double p-ks* (preacher's kids). She and I worked in separate churches and then as co-pastors until her early death at the age of fifty. Later I married Elizabeth Byers, daughter of a Presbyterian minister and denominational leader. She is a church elder, musician, and volunteer in her own right, who had been widowed at about the same time as I had been. We continue together as dedicated servants of churches we are related to in our retirement years.

I am grateful for my childhood grounding in faith in the Okaton Church, its Sunday School, the missionary speakers, and the daily family Bible readings. It was a solid foundation. I learned the stories of the Old and New Testament. I experienced God, salvation, and assurance of eternal life. But as I look back, I am equally grateful for the many lessons I have continued to learn along the way.

For example, African American Christians, whose communities still suffer from racial discrimination and injustice, read the biblical stories with different eyes than my childhood mentors. I have grown to appreciate how the messages of the Old Testament prophets, Jesus' words of hope and new life, and his deeds of healing have helped sustain those communities through hard times. The life work of Jesus and the prophets of Israel are, for the Black community, much more immediately relevant to their lives than St. Paul's teachings on eternal life.

I am also deeply grateful for my experiences with Native Americans, in the Arctic and the Laguna Pueblo in New Mexico, where I have led worship several times a year in retirement. These communities have practiced mutual sharing for untold generations and still have much to offer the rest of the world if we can learn to hear their wisdom. I have also led worship occasionally in small Hispanic American churches of northern New Mexico with long legacies of serving their communities with education and health care. As their communities and opportunities change, they struggle to continue their ministries much as the Okaton Church has done.

I have come a long way from the songs and sermons of my childhood, and yet I can trace who I am from those roots. It has been a continuous and positive journey.

This picture of the Okaton Reformed Congregation was indeed taken
in 1957, but it was in late summer, not fall as labeled. My mother
took the initiative, as she typically did, to arrange for the photo. She
wanted to be sure it was taken before we moved to Oregon. I am in
the picture, and since I left for Oregon in early September to start
school, the picture was taken before that—probably in August. It is
a little larger group than usual. Several visitors in the picture would
have been there on August vacations. All the farmers were there; they
would not take a vacation in August! A print of this photo still hung
in the back of the church more than 60 years later. Our whole family
is in this picture—my head is at the corner of the left window, and
my brother Gene is next to me, already slightly taller than I was.

THIRTEEN

Learning Begins

With the ongoing additions and modifications to our home, and an ever-shifting array of clergy leading worship in our church, I might have remembered our life as being in constant flux. Yet what I actually remember is a constancy—a predictability to life on the windblown plains of South Dakota. Much of the prairie was "broken" for farming, while some remained "unbroken," but there was a sense that everything would remain as it always had been.

The seasons came and went unvaryingly. Time moved slowly, but everything seemed to be in its place. On Sundays we sometimes sang a hymn that summed it up nicely:

> Great is Thy faithfulness," O God my Father,
>> There is no shadow of turning with thee. . .
> Summer and winter, and springtime and harvest,
>> Sun, moon, and stars in their courses above,
> Join with all nature in manifold witness
>> To Thy great faithfulness, mercy, and love. (Thomas O.
Chisholm, 1923)

We saw yellow cowslips and bluebells every spring shortly after the ground thawed. The redwing blackbirds perched on our fence. Meadowlarks lifted their beautiful notes to be heard above the sound of any motor vehicle we were riding in. The strength of their song affirmed nature's immutability. The flowers and birds were predictable, and so were the people. They got dusty and sweaty working in the summer heat but were always clean on Sunday. Everyone was scratching an existence out of the shallow South Dakota gumbo. Although we weren't exactly a part of nature, we were close to it, and it was neither mysterious nor foreign.

Some years were good for the farmers, and some were not. When we had a bountiful crop, we might get a new car, truck, or tractor. In bad years we made do with what we had. We were never hungry and didn't consider ourselves poor. Great quantities of fresh garden vegetables grown with irrigation from our dam were a joy of summer, and much was preserved for the winter. Mom and the other women took pride in the jars of green beans, tomatoes, or cucumber pickles they had canned during the season. Home raised beef, pork, and chicken were always in our home or stored in the locker plant in Murdo. We were never without eggs and milk. We always had plenty to eat in all seasons.

My perception of our stable environment and our church life taught me not to expect change. When I was five or six, about to enter first grade, I was shocked to hear that two young neighbors were about to be married. I had known both of them well, especially the man. He was about fifteen years older than me and that much younger than Dad. He had worked with my father, who had also become his farming mentor. I couldn't believe that he would be getting married. I didn't want to see anything change. It wasn't that I knew nothing of weddings; I clearly remembered the marriage of my Aunt Gertrude in Grandpa and Grandma's living room. I was one of the little kids who sat on the floor at the feet of the bride and groom as they said their vows. Her wedding hadn't seemed out of place to me, but for some reason the marriage of our young neighbors was another thing. It threatened to upset the unchangeable order of my world.

I thought about the world as a small child and as I grew older. Sometimes I wondered about the machines we used on the farm as well as the conveniences we were beginning to have in our home. Were modern inventions tampering with the world God had given us? Did God like cars and tractors or the large earthen Oahe Dam that was being planned for the Missouri River near Pierre? When God created the world and called it good, did God expect us to make "improvements" in it? Feeling safe with consistency, I wrestled with the changes that were taking place. Even though I was excited by new cars, new machines, and the opportunities to use them, I didn't really want life to change very much. I was a comfortably conservative farm kid.

Yet, while I was young, trying to understand my world, I was fascinated by complexity—although I didn't know that word. Two situations remain vivid in my memory, one at church and one on the farm. Hearing Rev. John Nyhoff preach before I started first grade at the age of six and a half, I remember his weekly sermons as being very long. Surely, he was a deep thinker, but all I can remember of his sermons were strings of big words that I found incomprehensible. One phrase that seemed meaningless to me at the time, but is vivid in my memory, was "the operation of the Holy Spirit." He must have said that often as I sat on the hard wooden chairs hearing him but engaging in more interesting mental diversions. As Rev. Nyhoff kept stringing long words into sentences, I finally concluded that adults could put all sorts of big words together, and they would mean something to them because they wanted them to, even if they didn't seem to make sense to me. I didn't call it magic, but in my thinking it was magical.

Another experience at about the same time was more engaging and maybe even more complex. It had to do with observing combines that had come into use long before I was born. The machine was so named because it combined the several harvest processes, from cutting the grain stalks to threshing out the wheat. In ancient times the cutting had been done with a scythe, but more recently it was accomplished by a reaping machine (or binder) that cut, bundled, and tied the grain stalks into sheaths. For millennia, including biblical times, hooved animals had trodden grains on a smooth surface to remove kernels from husks. The human activity of winnowing followed—allowing the wind to separate the grain from the chaff. In the early 1900s large threshing machines had replaced those ancient methods. Then advent of the combine eliminated the necessity of sheathing the grain and transporting it from the field. One complicated contraption combined the task of threshing with the other harvest tasks as it moved through the field.

When I was young, Dad had a small International Harvester combine that got its energy for threshing from the power take-off of his John Deere tractor that pulled it. Later he purchased a larger Gleaner Baldwin combine with its own engine, but still pulled by a tractor. But because of the urgency of the annual harvest, when the time came, assistance was welcomed. Custom combining crews followed the wheat harvest from early summer to early autumn starting in Oklahoma or Texas and working their way up into Saskatchewan and Alberta. Their large, self-propelled Massey Harris machines were pulled behind big grain trucks on the highways as they moved from one harvest location to the next.

Little kids were forbidden to get close to any working combines, but from a safe distance we could easily see how complicated they were. We could see parts going back and forth, and around and around all over them. What were all of those things doing? Wheels and pulleys, chains and belts, shakers and movers—it was as hard to understand, and even more fascinating than Rev. Nyhoff's sermons. But it became clear to me that adults were somehow able to stick all of those mechanical things together and make them do what they wanted done. There was much magic in a combine.

I remember vividly the similarity of the complexity of the sermons and of the combines. I am not sure when I put the two experiences together, but in my memory, they are one. I was only beginning to understand everything in the world.

I clearly remember when I learned certain things. Once Dad commented on the publication date of something he was reading, and I asked, "How can you tell what year that was done?" He opened the book and showed me the date. He went on to explain that the year we were in was 1948. I was surprised, but if I hadn't learned about the sequence of years, I would not have appreciated the significance of the approaching new decade. When we entered the 1950s, the milestone seemed momentous to me—maybe even more so than the new millennium was to seem fifty years later.

Of course, I learned all the things required in my years in school. But I will never forget a first-grade experience when a fellow student, a few grades ahead of me, taught me something I hadn't gotten to in class. Joyce Blair demonstrated the classroom's mechanical model of the solar system. The golden sun was in the middle, and the little earth on a wooden arm swung around it. The even smaller moon, on a piece of heavy wire hung around the earth. She explained to me that the earth revolves around the sun, and the moon revolves around the earth. I didn't want to believe her at first; the flat earth with the sun and moon going around it seemed easier to accept. But eventually she convinced me it was true. In my early years I had begun to grasp something that human beings had puzzled over for eons.

But there was still much for me to learn.

FOURTEEN

Our First Smoke

On a Fourth of July in the early 1950s, my cousin Richard and I sat under a cottonwood tree at the edge of a dry creek—two little boys trying to light a cigar!

As early as I can remember, my cousin and I saw a lot of each other. Richard is two years older than I. He lived with his parents, two brothers, and three sisters in a tiny farmhouse not far from ours. We saw each other on Sundays at church and were the only boys in our age group. When I started school at age six, Richard was already in the third grade. We were in the same room and began to see each other daily. I'm not sure we were best friends, but Richard tolerated me—a younger cousin—as somebody to play with. I enjoyed his company and looked up to him.

The differences between Richard and me were more pronounced than just the two years that separated us. He seemed so calm: I was amazed by how still he could sit during the church services, not fidgeting as I always was. He also seemed meticulous in the way he did things— how he folded the weekly Sunday School papers. Mine always got rolled up and had frayed ends from being in my mouth, but Richard's were always carefully folded to precisely fit into his pocket. I couldn't understand how anyone could do that.

A big event in our community was the Sunday School Fourth of July picnic. It was always held in a hay field or cow pasture—that year it was a pasture. There was nothing particularly religious about the picnic, except for our grandfather Henry Roghair's long prayer before we were allowed to eat the sumptuous potluck meal. The moms got up early to prepare fried chicken, potato salad, pies, and all sorts of goodies from our farms and gardens. We would all overeat.

That year, my brother Gene and I were old enough to be on our own for the day, and we each got a dollar or two to spend at the picnic concession stand. It was an open structure of rough planks, nailed together with a galvanized water tank in the center—the kind used for watering cattle. Either new or cleaned up for the picnic, it was filled with icy water to keep the soda pop cold until sold. Also for sale were candy, firecrackers, and other assorted items. Dad, or one of our uncles, would staff the stand together with someone from the other large family in the church.

Although we rarely had pop in our home, and what we did have was parceled out sparingly, our parents indulged us kids to drink as much pop as we wanted on the day of the picnic. They also didn't closely supervise how we spent our allowances for the day. What kind of trouble could we get into at the Sunday School picnic—except to get sick from overconsumption?

I don't know whether Richard's parents were as lenient about what their kids bought as ours were. Nor do I remember which of us came up with our plan, or whose dime we used. But at the ages of about ten and eight, Richard and I bought an El Roi-Tan Cuban cigar. Our Uncle Albert actually sold it to us. The tallest of my dad's siblings, at about six foot four inches, and very slender, Albert always had a twinkle in his eye, as if he were about to tell a joke. We knew we had to pay close attention to determine whether he was telling us the truth or a tall tale. He challenged us kids to think and to take some risks.

When he sold it to us, I'm not sure whether Albert knew our plan for the cigar. Surely, he thought of the sale as a joke and was curious to see what would happen. Would these two foolish nephews get sick from smoking the cigar? Wouldn't that be a good lesson to keep them from becoming smokers? Whatever he might have thought, he sold us the tobacco.

Richard and I didn't intend to smoke the cigar, but instead to use it as punk to light the fuses of our firecrackers. We wouldn't have to strike so many matches. Pieces of slow-burning punk with wire handles for lighting firecrackers were for sale at the time, but no punk was stocked in the picnic stand. So, our idea was practical and inventive—just how farm kids are supposed to be. We had learned to *make do* from our elders.

I wonder if Albert expected us to get the cigar lit. We knew that a match held to the end of punk would light it. We didn't understand that we had to draw air into the cigar to get it going. Had we gotten it lit and inhaled real smoke, we likely would have become sick, but we weren't successful. Although our adult uncle had been part of our scheme, we knew that we weren't really supposed to have a cigar. We wanted to make our cigar punk work, but we couldn't risk asking for any. adult help. Nobody missed us, since they were all watching the annual baseball game between the married men and the singles. But when we couldn't make the cigar burn, we finally gave up and threw it away—a wasted dime. It was at least twenty years before I actually smoked and probably about the same for Richard.

In retrospect it seems odd that cigars were even for sale at our picnic. Hardly anyone in the family smoked, although I think Grandpa might have lit up a cigar from time to time. There was rarely even a cigarette in the extended family or church community. So who was expected to buy cigars at the picnic?

Indeed, what was in Albert's mind when he agreed to sell us the cigar? Was it his responsibility to corrupt his nephews—just a little? We weren't his kids. They weren't born yet, so they were in no danger from cigars. But I have wondered over the years, did Albert ever give any of his own three children a cigar? Whose responsibility would it have been to corrupt Albert's kids—just a little?

FIFTEEN

Learning to Drive

Lesson One

Every child has reasons for wanting to grow up. I wanted to drive. Big people were always driving. In reality, maturing was much more complex than I could have imagined as a boy. Adulthood crept into my life at its leisurely pace, and it was hard to tell when I really got there. But learning to drive was more abrupt.

Driving lessons–informal as they were–began in 1947 when Dad brought home one of the first Willys Jeeps in Jones County. This was the four-wheel drive vehicle built for the US Army in World War II. Dad's Jeep was not army surplus, but an early civilian benefit of war-sparked ingenuity. It was a close replica of the Army model with one exception. Instead of drab green, it sported a more cheerful red paint. It was equipped with two front seats behind the windshield. Wheel well covers in the back served as two inward facing, unpadded seats for up to four kids, just as they would have for young soldiers in far off places. It had a canvas top and back, and its canvas front doors had flexible plastic windows on either side. Doors, cover, and back were all removable, although only the back was ever removed from our Jeep every summer.

I was only four when the Jeep arrived and became one of our major modes of transportation. Its simplicity and compactness made it easy for an interested child to study, imagine, and figure out how to drive it. That is what I did as soon as it joined our household.

When I was five or six, I made my first attempt at driving. Dad had pulled the Jeep up toward the tiny wood frame building serving at the time as the Okaton Post Office. The bare ground on which he parked slanted upward toward the building. Dad stopped the engine, put the transmission in reverse or first gear so the engine would be the brake, and left the key in the ignition, but he did not set the hand brake. Why set the brake? The engine would hold it. Dad got out and told us to wait for him. My brother Gene, two years younger, was in the back. Our sister Crysti was very small and not with us that day.

I sat in the front passenger seat while Dad went to check the mailbox. As was his habit, he got into an extended conversation with one of our neighbors. They all met at the Post Office. Although waiting for Dad always seemed like a long time, it surely wasn't too long. But it was just enough time for me to slip over into the driver's seat and put my small foot on the clutch. Suddenly the Jeep was rolling backwards. I was scared and not wise enough to take my foot off the clutch pedal to stop the roll.

Just as the Jeep started to roll, our family friend and neighbor, Russell Tedrow, came out of the Post Office. He saw what was happening, and in seconds jumped into the driver's seat pushing me over to take control. We were stopped, and safe. No harm was done.

When Dad appeared, tall and lean in his striped overalls, he took charge of his Jeep and his kids. His countenance was grim, but characteristically, he didn't say anything. Dad did not express anger verbally. Yet even at my age, I could feel the pressure as we drove away. What was coming next?

I sensed something had to be done to break the icy silence, so I started a conversation. Our neighbor's face, as he came out of the Post Office toward us, was imprinted in my mind, so I said, "Dad, don't you think Mr. Tedrow looks like a Jap?" It was only a few years after the war, and what I said reflected common language I had heard. Russell wasn't Asian, but he had high cheekbones and a high forehead, Eastern European ancestry, perhaps, and he reminded me of pictures of Asians I had seen.

I soon knew the conversation I started wasn't working for me, but it gave Dad something to respond to. "I'll Jap you," he said, "if you ever do anything like that again!" Often Dad didn't bother to be precise with words, but his meaning was absolutely clear. There was no further lecture, and I never did that again. Nor did I ever again use the racial epithet.

Thus ended my first driving lesson.

Lesson Two

I remember no further driving experiments. But, as I was getting a little older, I started paying close attention to the mechanics of driving. The episode at the Post Office became a distant memory for both of us, and as we rode together, Dad made a point of talking about what he was doing as I watched him drive. I began to "get the hang of it." I was, however, totally surprised one summer day when I was eight. We were nearly half a mile from our farmhouse with both the tractor and the Jeep. The entire road home was visible from where we were. What Dad said seemed to come totally out of the blue, but had likely been rehearsed in Dad's mind for quite some time. He said, "You get in and drive the Jeep home. I'll bring the tractor."

He positioned me in the driver's seat, reached over to make sure the two small levers to the right of the floor gear shift were positioned in low range and four-wheel drive, for the slowest possible transmission speed. He then told me to step on the clutch while he shifted the transmission into gear. "You can drive home in first gear," he said. With no other instruction, I was off. Driving!

I knew about the clutch and the brake, but as I was creeping home, I couldn't remember how I was supposed to stop. So when I arrived at the fence around the house, mine wasn't the smoothest stop. I jammed my foot on the brake and killed the motor–like many new drivers before and after me. But the Jeep was on the home place. I had driven home, and I stood several inches taller–on my way to adulthood.

That was my second driving lesson, but only the beginning of my driving adventures.

Lesson Three

I had experiences operating tractors, our farm truck, and our Ford car in the next few years. When I was thirteen, Dad took me to Murdo to get South Dakota driving permits to drive on the highway to and from school and anywhere in the State for farm-related purposes. South Dakota did not offer drivers' licenses for adults in those days. Anyone sixteen could drive legally, but thirteen-year-olds could be tested and get special permits.

Dad left me at the County Courthouse with the State patrolman and went off to tend to some business. I filled out the required paperwork and the officer was ready to give me a road test. He asked what kind of car I was used to driving. I didn't think to say that I had hardly ever driven a car but usually a Jeep. Instead, I said, "We have a 1949 Ford." He surprised me by saying, "Then you can drive my car."

Trembling, I got behind the wheel of the State cruiser to take my road test. I drove around the county seat for the first time ever. I was so nervous I ran the stop sign near the grain elevator. But the officer approved me anyway, and I received the two restricted permits.

With the school permit I could legally drive between our home and the school, but not take a two-block side trip to the Post Office. On the other hand, with the farm permit I might have driven a truck with several tons of grain all the way across the State, as long as I was on agricultural business. Of course, Dad was more cautious than the State, and I was not allowed to use the agricultural permit for anything dangerous.

Yes, I was now a driver. But I was still far from being a grown-up.

This was the first driving excursion I was allowed to take. I drove
Gene and Crysti to Grandpa and Grandma's house to see our new
aunt Zelda. She had recently married our uncle Ted. It was 3½ miles
on dirt roads—not the highway. I had no drivers permit at the time.

SIXTEEN

Learning to Swim

Some people learn to swim as infants or little kids. For them swimming seems to come naturally, or at least smoothly. But I became a swimmer by fits and starts. Along the way I learned a number of unrelated but valuable life lessons. Finally, after trying for six years, I actually did learn to swim.

Lesson One, Swimming in the Dam

In the semi-arid climate of western South Dakota, the water of the dam near our house loomed large in our daily lives. It covered several acres and was at least ten feet deep at its center, but with unpredictable deep spots all over its sticky gumbo mud floor. On summer afternoons, it was not surprising that we children clamored to get into the water, nor that our parents were cautious. Neither of them could swim. Nonetheless, on those hot days, the water seemed irresistible.

My first lesson in swimming came on such an afternoon in 1948. I was five, and my brother Gene was three. Mom had cut off our worn jeans above the knees, and they were our "swimming suits." We eagerly went "swimming"–actually it was only wading, because we had yet to learn anything beyond that. I distinctly remember Mom's orders, "Don't get your pants wet."

107

At the time, our sister Crysti was a toddler, just one year old. Wearing a diaper, she came into the water with us. I don't remember Mom's instructing her to stay in the shallow water nor me to watch her. Fully clothed and wearing her shoes, Mom watched us from the shore. I was minding my own business, wading in the shallow water with mud up to my ankles, when Mom started shouting at me. I didn't understand why. I looked down to make sure I hadn't gotten my pants wet.

Before I had more time to think, Mom came running into the water, shoes and all. Crysti had wandered off toward the deep water. Mom had assumed that I, only a few yards away, would recognize my sister's danger and protect her. But I was concentrating on my pants. Crysti was rescued, and no harm was done. But for the next sixty years, I was teased, first by my mom and later by Crysti; they retold the story that I had done nothing to save my own sister from drowning.

I now understand why Mom, aware of the danger of the water, gave her instructions about keeping our pants dry. If we didn't go out to the deep water, we wouldn't drown. Not going in deeper than the legs of our cut-offs was a rule for our own safety, but I had assumed it was about the pants. Trying to follow the rules, I missed the larger responsibility of an older brother to look out for his little sister's safety.

That experience became my first lesson in swimming: adults don't only mean what they say—they may expect more. So, you can't get by just doing what you are told. I had kept my pants dry, but I was still in trouble.

Lesson Two, Classes in Aberdeen

The summer I was nine, Mom and her oldest sister Frances Storm—Aunt Franny—hatched a scheme: I would visit her, Uncle Leonard, and my two older cousins, Geri and Linda in Aberdeen, South Dakota. I would take one week of swimming lessons at the YMCA, and I would learn to swim.

This was a memorable adventure for me. I had never ridden a bus before, so it was a big experience to travel by myself on the Jackrabbit bus line about two hundred and fifty miles from Murdo to Aberdeen. We waited for the coach at the edge of Okaton and followed it to the café in Murdo that served as a bus stop. The route was east to Huron–about half the trip–then a change of buses to go north to Aberdeen. Dad instructed the bus driver so he would understand what I was supposed to do, and then told me, "When you get to Huron, get off the bus and follow the driver. He will show you where to catch the bus to Aberdeen."

It all worked out. In Huron there was even time for me sit next to the driver and order my favorite café meal. That was an open-faced roast beef sandwich on white bread with mashed potatoes all smothered in gravy and green beans on the side. I would order the same meal whenever I ate in a restaurant, which wasn't too often.

On the trip north, I looked out the bus window at the familiar prairie and wheat land and read a "Donald Duck" comic book. Before we reached Aberdeen, it had become too dark to read. Aunt Franny and my two cousins were there to meet the bus, and Uncle Leonard was at home when we arrived. They welcomed me warmly, and I spent Saturday night and Sunday with them before the swimming classes started on Monday.

My aunt drove me to the class every morning that week. The experience at the Y was all new to me. I had never seen an indoor swimming pool before, nor had I ever taken a shower. I hadn't been in a crowd of so many boys my own age, and I didn't know any of them. The swimming pool was frighteningly noisy and chaotic. Chlorine mist filled my nostrils. Some of the boys in the pool were nude–something I had not expected. I was the little nine-year-old country boy, and no one talked to me.

The instructors shouted orders to us that echoed in the big room. Nothing about the experience was conducive to my learning. When I arrived late the second day the instructors shouted at me, even though I tried to repeat what Aunt Franny had said, "Tell them the alarm clock didn't work this morning."

The biggest obstacle, and one that I did not overcome, was that

I was terrified to put my head under the water. No one gave me any assistance. Swimming in the dam without getting my pants wet had been no preparation. I had had little other experience in water. The square galvanized tub in which we took our weekly baths was less than three feet across—not even big enough to lie down and let the water cover my ears. I had never tried to put my nose under water. But the instructors expected us all to do it the first day. Since I couldn't master putting my head in the water, the swimming classes were a bust. By Friday I was glad they were over. The only important thing I gained from the classes was a determination to learn to put my head under water.

While I was visiting in Aberdeen, my aunt took me to visit Bobby, a neighbor boy my age who lived in a large home. She made the point that his family was the richest in Brown County. It seemed important to her to connect with the upper crust, and she often identified her own husband as having the biggest farm in the county. But there was nothing ostentatious about the way her own family lived—modestly on the edge of town in a rented house. They had indoor plumbing, but also an outhouse.

I was duly impressed by my visit to Bobby's home. He had a bedroom of his own. It was filled with toys and games that he let me play with. I had an enjoyable afternoon with him.

When I got back home, I was eager to share all my adventures. I echoed my aunt's words about the wealth of Bobby's family. I must have said they were the richest people in Brown County one time too many. In agitation Dad answered, "I don't want to hear anything more about Bobby's family," and I never mentioned them in Dad's presence again. He was never impressed by people because they were wealthy, and he didn't want me to be, either.

I didn't learn to swim in Aberdeen that summer. But not only did I learn that I had to put my head down into the water if I was going to swim, I also learned that I had to keep my head up around people of wealth.

Lesson Three, Swimming at Last

For several years I practiced putting my face in water every time I had a chance. Shortly after we had moved to Oregon, I was fifteen and had started high school, when I finally did learn to swim. Mom's family was picnicking July Fourth 1958 in the McMinnville city park. Mom's brother Clifford Bowder rounded up a carload of cousins from the picnic to go to another park with a big outdoor pool.

As I was about to get into the water, Uncle Cliff, as we called him, asked me if I knew how to swim. When I said I didn't, he sat down on the concrete edge of the pool and instructed me. He carefully explained and demonstrated the process: I should lean my head on my left arm and turn to the right to breathe while my left arm was extended. Then I should put my face into the water and draw my left arm down and back while I extended the right. I should repeat the arm movements and breathing, all the while kicking my feet up and down. It worked. To my amazement I had learned the crawl. I was swimming!

The key to my learning was the careful, logical and patient explanation of my uncle. I never became a really good swimmer, but in later years I have enjoyed this healthy exercise. Often, I consider how Cliff's ability to articulate and demonstrate the steps facilitated my own learning so much more effectively than the impersonal group lessons I had taken years earlier in Aberdeen. I came to realize that my personality and learning style made it easier for me to learn from the "thinking" approach Cliff offered. Many years later at Cliff's memorial service, I was surprised to hear my brother Gene and several of our cousins say that Uncle Cliff had taught each of them to swim, too.

The process of becoming a swimmer was circuitous. It didn't happen the way my mom or aunt thought it might, but in my own time I did learn. The other outcomes of my swimming lessons, however, were more important than the water skill: taking responsibility beyond the stated rules, recognizing the equality of people regardless of social standing, and finally recognizing that each of us has our unique way of learning.

SEVENTEEN

Okaton School

The *1950 Okaton Bulldog*, the school yearbook, dedicates three of its thirty numbered pages to the men's basketball squad. On one page are individual pictures of each of the twelve players wearing their jerseys. Two of them caught my attention: my cousin, Melvin Roghair, and a neighbor, Dickie Daum. Not mentioned in the narrative is that these two were seventh graders whose playing made it possible for the high school, with only ten male students, to launch a men's basketball squad of twelve. They often played both A and B games on the same nights. It must have been quite an experience for those two to be welcomed onto the high school team.

The other thing not mentioned in the *Bulldog* write-up is a description of the basketball court itself where the team practiced and played. With a ceiling barely over ten feet high and hanging water pipes connected to radiators in the rooms above, the height of the court was a bit below standard. The baskets were hung at about eight and a half feet. Perhaps that made it easier for the players to hit layups, but it did not give much room for the arc of a long shot. (The 3-point shot had yet to be invented.) Of course, the length of the room was another issue. It was so short that the faded white paint of the free-throw circles at either end of the court intersected, not only with the jump circle in the middle, but also with many irregular cracks in the gray concrete floor.

It wasn't much of a gym, but, accustomed to it, the Okaton team had the legendary home court advantage and won their two home games that year. The five away games were all losses. Likely the other squads had never tried to play in a "cracker box," as Okaton residents affectionately called our little gym, and the Okaton team had no opportunity to practice on a court whose dimensions were closer to the regulations.

Although I was in the first grade in the 1949-50 school year, I was unable to be a spectator at any of the games. There wasn't much room for non-players. The court had walls on three sides about a yard from the boundary lines, so all spectators occupied the little stage behind the basket at only one end. Of course, the gym served many purposes—a place for the elementary kids to play during recess in bad weather, a theater for school plays and community talent shows, an auditorium or meeting room for community groups and events, and the polling place on election days. It wasn't a grand room but was the only community space we had except the churches.

The gym was in what we called the basement, really a scant half story below ground level, so there were windows for natural light near the ceiling of the room on one side. That lower level of the building also had a manual training room with woodworking tools, as well as a hallway with a drinking fountain, that someone had to fill from time to time since there was no running water. There was a small table near it that might have had a wash basin, but I can't remember washing my hands there. The girls' and boys' toilets were accessed off the hallway. They were only a slight improvement over the outhouses we all had at home. The toilets had modern-looking seats but did not flush. A pit under the floor was connected to a cesspool. The sludge, regularly treated with some chemical to ameliorate its odor, slowly made its way underground away from the building. Perhaps someone brought water to add and keep things moving, but I didn't observe such maintenance.

The furnace room in the corner of the building was behind the stage and next to the boys' restroom. Coal, shoveled in through the coal-chute, fired the boiler that fed hot water to the classroom radiators. The cinders were discarded in the back yard and became a knee-skinning hazard for students as we played recess games. There wasn't much reason for us to be in the furnace room, but I do remember a cold day in first grade when the heat in our classroom was not working, and we spent the morning huddled around the furnace with our teacher reading us stories. I don't remember ever seeing any maintenance of the heating system, although it must have taken considerable effort to keep it fueled with coal and working properly.

The high school boys surely found the coal-chute a convenient entrance into the building after it was locked up on Halloween night 1949. When everyone arrived at school the following day there was a wide variety of junk in the hallway between the classrooms upstairs—most notably an old horse carriage (without the horse), and an old kitchen range. It was a great trick that had taken much work to accomplish. The superintendent wanted to investigate who was responsible and make them do the clean-up. My uncle Jack, who was president of the school board at the time, advised the superintendent to require all the high school boys to do the clean-up. Jack either knew or suspected that they had all been involved, including his two youngest brothers. The clean-up was completed and no boy that I know of protested his innocence.

When I started first grade, the building was fully occupied. All four of the regular classrooms were on the upper floor, a half story above ground. Our primary room had grades one to four, and the grammar room, five to eight. The other two were high school rooms, one of which was designated the typing room. Across from the stairway and adjoining the high school rooms was a tiny room that served as the superintendent's office and the school library.

115

The building's main entrance was a double door into an entry room with bins on two walls for overshoes. An opposite double door opened onto the landing, with stairs to go up or down half a story. On the left side of the stairs leading up was a smooth, shiny wooden banister about six inches wide. There were parent and teacher rules against sliding down the banister, but it was irresistible. When no adult was watching we would slip onto it face down and slide to the bottom. As we got a little older and braver, we sat on the banister face out with arms extended to slide down—an action that seemed to require a bit of a sound like, "Whee!"

When I was in first grade, my two youngest uncles, Ted and Bob, were high school juniors, cousins Lorraine and Melvin were in the grammar room in grades six and seven, and three cousins were in the primary room with me, Lawrence in fourth grade, Richard in third, and Alice Mae in first with me. Counting the pictures in the 1950 yearbook, I see that we Roghairs were seventeen percent of the school (seven out of forty-two) that year.

Okaton School was one of Jones County's town schools, the others being in Draper and Murdo. The three towns in our county were spaced evenly along the Milwaukee Railroad when it was built in 1906, and US Highway 16, built in the 1940s, paralleled the track through each town. There were fewer than a hundred residents in Okaton in 1949. I remember that in the mid-1950s my brother Gene and a man called Swede sat in the café and did an informal, but highly accurate census, of the town. Their count was sixty-three. It didn't take the two of them much time or effort to tabulate the population, since we all knew everyone. Gene had just delivered the week's *Grit* (which called itself *America's Greatest Family Newspaper*) to half the town and collected a dime for each paper. I was finishing up the other half. Swede and his wife operated the gas station and café on the new 1950s Highway 16 which passed alongside the townsites, rather than going through them.

The white stucco school building was built before the depression of the 1930s but was reconditioned during the New Deal. It was well-designed to be a twelve-grade school. The Okaton district drew high school students from at least six other districts that each had typical one-room wood frame country schools with an outhouse. They were taught by one teacher covering eight grades—or at least all grades that had children. Some of the country schools were very small.

I had no idea when I started school what drastic changes were to take place in the school in the next few years. In my second year, 1950-51, according to that year's *Bulldog*, the Okaton school population dropped to twenty-nine, a thirty percent drop. By the following year 1951-52, the school board decided to close the high school and turn Okaton into a one-room school with one teacher. In the fall with seventeen pupils, it seemed like this new one-room plan was going to work, but circumstances quickly changed.

Okaton Public School from the *Okaton Bulldog, 1951*.

OKATON vs. WOOD

Basketball in the Crackerbox, from the *Okaton Bulldog,1950.*

EIGHTEEN

My Favorite Teachers in the Okaton School

During the eight school years from 1949 to 1957, Okaton School was a formative and central part of my life. I was taught by five different teachers. Each of them had her own unique experiences, imagination, and creativity to mold the life of the school. Those who impressed me the most were my first two, Miss Sloan and Mrs. Gilbert.

Miss Sloan

Miss Sloan, my first-grade teacher, was new to the community. When she greeted her students on the first day of school in September 1949, there were ten in her room, one in fourth grade, three in third, one second, and five in first. My cousins Lawrence, Richard, and Alice Mae and I were in her room—four Roghairs. Although at school we always addressed her as *Miss Sloan*, and that is how her picture is labeled in the school annual, I remembered her given name as *Molly*, but I recently discovered it signed as *Mary*. So, I am unsure what she went by. Since she was *Miss Sloan* to us, that is sufficient for this context.

Miss Sloan had a special way of engaging her students at our own level. She had recently completed her educational training and was ready to put to work the techniques she had recently learned. Everything in the classroom seemed as new and fresh for her as it was for us. With the small number of students in her room, she helped us arrange our desks in the shape of a banana. That made the room feel more inviting and fun, than the usual straight rows with students in front and back of each other. We were positioned more intimately with each other and our teacher. I remember how enjoyable it felt to be part of the banana.

For the first grade she prepared blue dittoed sheets that had outlines of grape clusters. As we completed assignments, we could color one grape purple for each reading or spelling lesson. With half her pupils in the first grade, she soon found it convenient to divide our class of five into two groups: the two boys, Clarence Rae and I, and the three girls, Alice Mae Roghair, Agnes Kleinsmith, and Mary Jo Kuckleberg. The boys seemed to be moving through the lessons a little faster than the girls, so it made a neat division, and she could give us more personal attention.

That year the grammar room teacher was Mrs. Quinn who was older than Miss Sloan. She had grades five through eight in her room of ten, including Lorraine and Melvin—two more of my Roghair cousins. Together the two teachers cooperated to organize a special program, something they called an operetta. Perhaps it was not true to the technical definition of the genre, and I have no idea what the plot of our show was. But it was fun. There was group singing; I remember "Sailing. Sailing, Over the Bounding Main," as Miss Sloan played the piano. I was cast as a firefly. Mom had made my costume out of blue crepe paper with gold paper between my arms and waist. As I flapped my wings the yellow showed. That costume was all I knew of fireflies until I was an adult—we never saw any at Okaton. Some of the girls were cast as flowers. Whether or not we understood our characters or even the story, all of the parents came to the program and were duly impressed by our performance and by the teachers' efforts.

Miss Sloan taught in Okaton one year, then married and moved to Rapid City. Like many children, I had fallen in love with my first-grade teacher. But I never saw or heard from her after that year, even though she had started me on an educational journey that would continue through several levels of higher education that my mom and dad encouraged.

Miss Sloan's experience was similar to my mother's when she had come to Okaton eight years earlier. Mom had just finished her training when she arrived, and her classroom included two Roghair brothers, Bob and Ted, in grades two and three. Mom had no inkling that they would become her brothers-in-law at the end of the school year (and eventually my uncles).

Mom had initially been amazed when she asked her second grader, Bob, to draw a picture of his family. She watched as he kept drawing more and more people—his eleven brothers and sisters and his parents. But it wasn't long before she got to know them all. She and Dad were married in June after Mom's year of teaching.

Their marriage set a precedent for Roghair men and new teachers. A few years later when I was a preschooler, Eva Lampert, with a master's degree in education, came to the Okaton School as Superintendent. I met her at our church as my first Sunday School teacher. It wasn't long before she married Uncle Albert.

So, when Miss Sloan arrived in 1949, the family took a good look at her. She was young and pretty, with long black hair and a pleasant personality—an eligible single. There was family gossip that she would be a good wife for my uncle Ted. He wasn't quite out of high school yet, and nothing came of that matchmaking. But there had been sufficient precedent for the idea to surface. Even though she did not become a part of our family, she remained a memorable first teacher for me.

Years later my oldest cousin, Melvin followed the precedent and married Clarice Caldwell who had come to teach at a rural one-room school near Okaton. Since Uncle Jack had become president of the school board of that rural district, and he had recruited Clarice to the school, she always maintained that Jack had chosen her to be his son's wife when he gave her the job.

Mrs. Lee Gilbert

By far the most creative of my teachers was Mrs. Lee Gilbert, who came as the primary room teacher in 1950 when I was in the second grade. The faculty she joined included a new male superintendent who also taught high school classes, one returning male high school teacher, and the returning female grammar room teacher. No one knew that this would be the final year of the high school. Its demise was decided in June 1951; the high school faculty had already been reduced to two from three the previous year. Okaton and its small surrounding districts would begin to send their students to Murdo, later to become the only high school in the county.

I don't know where Mrs. Gilbert had lived or taught before she came to our town; I had heard someone say she was French Canadian. Clearly Mrs. Gilbert came as an experienced teacher with her own ideas of what was important to teach and the methods to use. She was of slight build with dark hair and the mother of a pre-school son. Her husband moved to Okaton with her. He cut men's hair and did odd jobs while she became the prominent presence in the school.

In her first Okaton classroom there were eight pupils, one in first grade, three in second, one in third and three in fourth. An early project for Mrs. Gilbert that year was to engage us all with some old phonics books to make sure we learned the rules of spelling and sound—things that weren't in our more current curriculum. We learned rules such as, "I before *e*, except after *c*, or when it sounds like *a* as in *neighbor* or *weigh*." Mrs. Gilbert taught us the kind of rules that stick with a person through the years.

Early in the school year, above the blackboards on two walls she tacked up a row of forty 8½ by 11-inch black and white reproductions of famous European and American paintings. Two I remember were "The Gleaners" by Millet and "Whistler's Mother" by Whistler. It was a contest; in February we would be tested on the names of the paintings and the artists. Whoever got the most right would win a prize; my cousin Richard won. She later assisted us to order small prints of some paintings we especially liked. Life in Mrs. Gilbert's classroom was always inspiring.

I doubt that she imagined when she joined the faculty of four in 1950 that by the fall of 1951, she would be Okaton School's only teacher—no more local superintendent, no high school teacher, and no other elementary teacher to collaborate with. She would be on her own with seventeen pupils. That is how classes started in September 1951, but by November the enrollment had ballooned to twenty-six. Nine new children had enrolled. They were living in what we called the *trailer camp*, the temporary village of mobile homes belonging to the families of the construction workers finishing the upgrade of US Highway 16. In a short time, the school board decided to hire Mrs. Schroll, one of the trailer camp residents, as a second teacher. She took the primary classes after Thanksgiving and continued through the remainder of the school year.

Mrs. Gilbert survived that chaotic school year and the infamous blizzard in January 1952. She had a good time teaching the older children, and even mobilized them to continue the mimeographed school newspaper, *The Cosmic Ray*, that had been a high school project. It was an extraordinary learning experience for the upper grades.

By the fall of 1952, as I began fourth grade, she was ready for her third year at Okaton. The highway was completed; the construction crew and their trailer camp were gone. My cousins had moved to their new home and enrolled in the one-room Scovil school. Suddenly our school was much smaller, and once again Mrs. Gilbert was the only Okaton teacher, having only eleven students.

It was Mrs. Gilbert's year to shine. An early project that year was getting steel, buckle-on roller skates for all the students. They were ordered, and soon arrived. I'm not sure whether each family paid for their own skates—perhaps she had received a grant through the Young Citizen's League to buy them. However they were obtained, we all began to roll on our concrete gym floor, and to gain confidence as skaters.

But skating was only one plan she hatched up that year—I think the regular state-prescribed curriculum may have taken a bit of a hit. She organized the school into a "Drum Major Drill Team." We acquired uniforms, dark tops and white pants for the boys, and the opposite for the girls, white tops and dark skirts. Each of us wore an "Okaton" banner from right shoulder to left waist. We started practicing our routine with a recorded Sousa march played on the school's new 45-rpm record player. By early spring the Kleinsmith family had come back to Okaton after spending the winter in Oregon. Larry Kleinsmith, an accomplished eighth grade pianist, was able to play a Sousa march for us. We performed our marching routine at the county Young Citizens League convention in Murdo and then were invited to take it to the State convention in Pierre. That was a high point of Mrs. Gilbert's time in Okaton.

Besides her energy and creativity, Mrs. Gilbert had a deep sensitivity to her individual pupils and their needs. I remember vividly one of my first days in fourth grade. I was often a bit disruptive in the classroom— perhaps speaking out of turn. I don't exactly remember what I did, but I remember the teacher's response. In a gentle tone and in front of the whole classroom, she called me by name, using my familiar nickname, "Jimmy, you are in the fourth grade, now. You are one of the big kids, and you need to set an example for the younger ones."

It was well-placed encouragement. Did she recognize that I was at a point of thinking about my own spiritual life and how it related to everything else? I was growing up in our small Protestant community, and she was Catholic, but it seemed to me that her words in school related deeply to what I was hearing in my own church and feeling in my own life. I have always remembered that day as a part of my spiritual journey. Perhaps spiritual guide is an unexpected role for a public-school teacher, but Mrs. Gilbert often did the unexpected, and I deeply cherish the influence she had on my education.

We had a great year, yet by the time the next school year came, Mrs. Gilbert was gone, and we had a new teacher. Three years was a longer stint than most of the teachers managed in our school, and in the rural schools around us. I don't think she had raised animosity. Rather, it was the common practice in the area for teachers to move on. Some made the rounds of the relatively local schools. But Mrs. Lee Gilbert moved to Draper, the town school on the other side of the county, and she taught there for a few years. After that I lost track of her.

Okaton School end of year picnic near Mrs. Gilbert's house.
We all picked wild bluebells.

NINETEEN

As the School Changed

Students Come and Go

When I was in first grade there were five of us, but by the time I graduated from eighth grade I was the only one in my class. There was fluidity in our small community.

One of my first-year classmates, Mary Jo Kuckleberg, had dark curly hair. She lived in her family's apartment in the Okaton Depot of the Milwaukee Railroad, since her father managed the station. Mary Jo was in our school only that one year. Her father moved on to another position, and the new family in the depot had a daughter a year younger who enrolled in first grade the following year.

Clarence Rae was the one first grader I had not known until I met him at school. He lived on a cattle ranch several miles north of Okaton in a school district without enough children to have a teacher. Clarence's tuition was paid to the Okaton School by his home district. He stayed with his grandparents in their small farmhouse a mile or two east of Okaton. His grandfather was not well, and his grandmother was often seen operating farm machinery. It seemed strange to see an elderly woman making hay. After Clarence's year at Okaton School, two additional children of school age were available in his home district, and a small school was opened for the three students. Before he moved back to his parents' home, I visited Clarence at his grandparents' home for one overnight with.

By second grade my class had decreased to three. My two remaining classmates were my cousin Alice Mae Roghair and Agnes Kleinsmith. Alice was characteristically thin, as we Roghairs all were, with fine blonde hair in bangs and curls in the back. She lived about two miles east of Okaton, and Agnes lived almost directly across the road from her. Agnes's dark hair was always in long braids tied in white ribbons. She was the youngest of a large family whose father had been in the US Army in World War I. He had changed his name from Kleinschmidt to Kleinsmith to avoid mistaken identity while fighting in Europe.

In our second or third grade year, the Kleinsmith family began to spend winters in Mt. Angel, Oregon, so Agnes and her older brother were in Okaton only to begin and end the school years. By eighth grade they had moved to Oregon permanently. Meanwhile Alice Mae and her family moved a few miles north of Okaton in the spring of our third grade, and she, her sisters, and brothers swelled the enrollment of the rural Scovil School. Thus, my class went from five to one in eight years.

The Memorable 1951-52 School Year

My third-grade year, and brother Gene's first, was especially notable because for much of the year our teacher was Mrs. Schroll, recruited from the trailer camp when the enrollment grew fast due to the construction workers building the new highway. I don't remember her first name, and the only thing I have with her signature is signed Mrs. Lyle Schroll. I have good feelings about our time with her, but I can't recall much of what we did in the classroom. Her daughter Janice was in my class for those few months, and I enjoyed getting to know her—even communicated with her by mail after they moved back to the Rapid City area. But many other things happened that year besides the major disruption of shifting from a one-room to a two-room school.

My Uncle Clifford Bowder, Aunt Marjorie, and their little daughters, Marilyn and Jaqui, expected to make a brief visit with us as they were *en route* by car from their home in Salem, Oregon, to Boston to celebrate Christmas 1951. A heavy snowfall in our area made the mile and a half trip from the highway to our farm questionable. Instead of turning off to our place, they went on into Okaton. People there, including some of Dad's family, advised them not to drive out to our farm. But Cliff was determined to see his sister and our family, so he did it anyway. After a day or two of visiting and Dad and Cliff's hard work digging his car out of the snow, the Bowders were finally on their way and arrived just in time to celebrate Christmas with Marjorie's family in Massachusetts.

This snowfall was a foretaste of even bigger weather events. A few weeks later the blizzard of 1952 stopped everything for several days and left our community stunned and grieving the death of neighbors. After that storm, Mom was afraid of more weather-related disasters. She made arrangements for Gene and me to stay in town for two or three weeks—Monday through Friday—at the home of our parents' friends, the Kesslers. They had two preschool boys who enjoyed having us as guests. Their house was large, and many years later I learned that it had once been the dormitory for Okaton School students who couldn't come and go daily.

In late April 1952, Grandpa and Grandma Bowder drove from Salem, Oregon, to be with us before and after the birth of our new brother Wallace in early May. Just before his birth, the Missouri River flooded, and the water almost reached the St. Joseph's Hospital in Pierre where he was to be born. There was more water that spring than the white population had ever seen or expected—all from the thaw of the huge winter snowfalls. (It was unsubstantiated, but I heard that a Lakota elder had warned early settlers that the river would become two squaws deep at Pierre, which it surely did that year!)

As the flooding subsided, Grandpa Bowder, always ready to make a dollar, got a job helping an amateur collector in Pierre clean up and sort out his Native American relics, buffalo hides, crafts, and other assorted soaked items. Perhaps as part of his payment, Grandpa was given a worthless, water-damaged piano. He borrowed Dad's two-wheeled trailer to bring it to our barn where it sat for years. It was never put to any use— not for music or even for materials to reuse—and it was still sitting in its place there when we moved away.

That same spring my five Roghair cousins who were still in the Okaton School moved into their new home and enrolled in their rural Scovil school. With 1951-52 being such a chaotic year, is it any wonder I don't remember much of what happened in school that year? It was perhaps best remembered as the lead-up to Mrs. Gilbert's really memorable final year in our school.

My Last Four Years of Grade School

In my final four years in the school, I had two teachers, Mrs. Martin and Mrs. Peters. Mrs. Edyth Martin was our teacher for my fifth, sixth and seventh grades. She had been making the rounds of the rural schools and had most recently been at the one-room Grandview School a few miles west of Okaton. Mrs. Martin's reputation was to give the most A's of any teacher in the county, which was good for my report card. She was an experienced teacher whose best subject was English. She taught me to diagram sentences. Sometimes I did the work on the blackboard, and she could watch what I was doing from her desk. I found sentence structure fascinating and learned it well.

But those three years in the school were also a time of ongoing struggle. By the time Mrs. Martin came, instead of the large coal-burning furnace in the basement an oil floor furnace was heating our individual classroom with a thermostat on the wall at the back of the classroom. Mrs. Martin was up in years, possibly beyond retirement age by that time, and she had the habit of turning the thermostat up to 80°—far too warm for the pupils.

By firth grade, I was the oldest boy in the school, and my seat was near the door in the back on the right side, farthest from the teacher's desk at the front left. Throughout the winter I would stand up from my desk, go to the pencil sharpener on the wall, and turning the handle, I surreptitiously pushed the thermostat down to 70°. Time and again the teacher recognized what I had done and came back to re-set the temperature. Alternatively, I would get up, go to the shelf by the door, pick up a dictionary, and quietly open the door to let in cold air from the hallway. I assume the other kids who were suffering from the heat appreciated my efforts, if they noticed. Only the coming of spring solved the thermostat problem.

My sister Crysti, in the first through third grades, was the teacher's darling. She reminded Mrs. Martin of her granddaughter, who had died. My brother Gene couldn't stand the teacher, so he always did the least amount of schoolwork required and spent the rest of his time educating himself by reading the encyclopedias that were in the hallway near the abandoned superintendent's office.

At the end of my seventh-grade year, I was supposed to receive a free ice cream cone from a store in Murdo because my report card had the highest number of A's in the county. Whether it was because of Mrs. Martin's reputation of giving high grades, or some other reason never revealed, I did not get the advertised prize. But I survived that disappointment: I was looking forward to my last year in Okaton School.

There wasn't much remarkable about my eighth-grade year, with Mrs. Helen Peters as teacher. I don't know how much education or teaching experience she had had, but she was one of the teachers making the rounds of the small schools in our area. There were some county requirements for grade school graduation which I did outside of school time. I submitted a leathercraft notebook I had made after learning how in Bible School, and I had already shown it at a 4-H achievement day. At Mom's suggestion, I had interviewed an early homesteader, Don Lobdell and my handwritten story fulfilled another requirement.

In the continual coming and going of our community, the Blair family, who lived in Okaton and for a time operated a café on old Highway 16, moved away taking several kids out of our school. But then a large Sioux family, the Crazy Bears, moved to Okaton and lived in the large home that had once been the dormitory for Okaton School students. The father was on the railroad section crew maintaining the track. Their five children added to the school's numbers, and the family brought racial diversity to our town.

At about the same time Dad's sister, my Aunt Janet (always pronounced *Janette*), and Uncle Bill Kelly, who had lived in a various places in South Dakota, moved back to Okaton for a few years. They adopted two sisters, Betty, a little older than me, and Bonnie, a little younger. Suddenly I had cousins in our school again. In the years after the trailer camp left, it was still exciting to have new pupils enroll whether they had just moved in or were the younger ones I already knew.

At the end of eighth grade our family was making plans to move to Oregon. I missed the County graduation ceremony in Murdo because we were on a trip to Oregon scouting out our options. Although the trip and the anticipated move were exciting, I was sorry to miss the program. I got my diploma in the mail.

In anticipation of high school, my slightly older cousins and friends warned me how hard it would be, "They grade on the curve!" I had little idea how the grades I had received were related to work I had actually done in school. In a class by myself for several years, there hadn't been any way to compare my work with anyone else's. So, when I looked forward to starting in a much larger high school, I didn't know what to expect.

When I did get to high school in McMinnville, Oregon, I soon recognized that my one-room education had served me well. In the first week of freshman English, the teacher was preparing to teach sentence structure—especially diagramming. He gave the class a pre-test, and then told me I could do something else for the first nine weeks; I already knew how to diagram sentences. I was surprised, but it clearly was an affirmation of my years in the Okaton School and especially what I had learned from Mrs. Martin.

TWENTY

How Was School Today?

A Day in the Classroom

My experiences in the Okaton School were affected by the skills, experiences, and personalities of the women who rotated though our district as our teachers. But how was a teacher's day in a one-room school? Regardless of how many of the individual eight grades actually had students, or how few pupils she had in any one grade, the teacher was always managing multiple tasks simultaneously. Normally she set aside certain times of the day or week for particular subjects. For example, everybody in the room was supposed to work on history for an hour or two at an assigned time. We were to read our lesson—perhaps several times. Within the schedule, we would be called up by grade for "recitation." We sat on a wooden bench facing the teacher's desk. It was our opportunity to discuss the lesson with the teacher, and she might ask us questions to judge how well we were learning.

Since this process was going on in the classroom continuously, I was often distracted by what other classes were doing. I could hear younger kids talking about what I had previously studied, and the older ones discussing things I was supposed to learn later. As a result, I had some trouble concentrating on my own lessons. I wasn't good at blocking out what I was hearing. But my brother Gene seemed to be more like our dad, shutting out what was going on around him. He would quickly finish his assignments so he could read the encyclopedias.

There were arithmetic assignments every day. Our textbooks had the answers in the back. The expectation was for us to write out our own work and then check the answers. If we had errors, we were supposed to keep working until we got everything right. For me, the arithmetic assignments usually took up more than the assigned time, and I was often still trying to finish the morning assignment near the end of the day.

Studying geography, we were sometimes assigned to draw a map of a state or a country—copying as best we could from a book. Occasionally we made "salt maps." Creating a substance of about equal parts of salt and flour, with enough water added to make a dough, we could shape a three-dimensional map of a geographical area. Mrs. Gilbert assigned salt maps for two compact mountainous countries, Switzerland and Ecuador. Working together with kids of other grades, it was great fun and an unforgettable way to learn.

Sometimes we didn't have regular textbooks for geography, and the most boring time I spent in school was trying to memorize facts outlined in the South Dakota curriculum manual. There were lists of the products of countries in South America, or the names of the capitals of African or Asian countries. I'm sure the manuals were not meant for memorization, but sometimes they were used that way. When a teacher had students in most or all of eight grades, she didn't have time to provide lectures, and sometimes she didn't have proper textbooks for us to read, so we studied the manual.

We took state-prescribed, printed tests every six weeks in a number of subjects. Sometimes the quizzes related to what we had actually been studying and sometimes they seemed unrelated. Often teachers would give us as much time as we needed to work through the tests. I think it was on an eighth-grade test, I was asked to convert a temperature reading from Fahrenheit to Centigrade. Probably the state curriculum assumed I had memorized the formula, but I didn't remember studying it. So, I spent considerable time working with what I did know: 0°C was 32°F, and 100°C was 212°F. Not having studied any algebra, it took me some time to work with fractions, addition, and subtraction to figure out the relationship of the two sets of degrees. I eventually did get the correct answer. I wonder, was that experience of impromptu calculation possibly of higher educational value than memorizing the formula?

Recess

We always looked forward to mid-morning and mid-afternoon recesses. They were the times when we pupils were relatively unsupervised for twenty minutes or more. We were outdoors during the warm weather of spring and fall. Often, we played what we called *baseball*, although we were really using a softball. We had a bat and some designated bases, but no gloves. The girls and boys all played together, and our teams included everyone—never conforming to any numerical regulation. No one was appointed umpire, so there could be no called balls, strikes, or walks. A strike was simply what happened when the hitter swung at a pitch and missed. The pitcher had to keep pitching until the batter physically struck out or hit the ball.

Usually, we had a good time playing our baseball with no official. But at times disagreements arose, not dissimilar to those of players and spectators in professional games with officials. People saw things differently: was a player safe or out? Was a hit in bounds or out? Our ball diamond was on rough prairie ground with native grasses and common weeds—even a small prickly pear cactus here and there. No markings on the ground clarified what was in or out of bounds so disagreements were complicated to resolve. Arguments sometimes became shouting matches and tempers flared—often pitting one family against another. When the teacher rang the hand bell to bring us back, she might have to spend classroom time trying to calm a baseball argument over a situation she had not even observed.

Although baseball was our most contentious recess activity, we often played other, less emotions-filled, games. We often played a tag game we called *cops and robbers*. Half of the kids would be cops and the other half robbers. The object was for the cops to tag the robbers, and then tagged, confine them to the jail, the stairwell leading down to the furnace room. The robbers could touch their fellows to tag them out of jail. If the recess was long enough, the cops and robbers exchanged places.

Part-way through my years in the school, a swing-and-slide set was installed. First it was located at the side of the building with no windows, but later it was moved to the front of the school, so the teacher could watch from her desk. Having this equipment gave kids the option of entertaining themselves rather than participating in the group activity of the day.

Most of the time boys and girls played together at recess, but sometimes we split up. One recess activity the boys did for a while was to bring in tiny toy Caterpillar tractors. Made at home out of chunks of wood an inch or two long and with no moving parts, they could be simply created with a saw and maybe a little whittling with a knife. Perhaps a bulldozer blade was nailed to the front. Farming was familiar to all of us, and we could spend recesses pretending to farm the loose dirt near the school. Other times the boys played marbles—not the game in which you would lose your marbles to a winner, but one in which the marbles were simply counted and returned to the one who brought them. I'm not sure what the girls did when the boys took up their special activities. Perhaps they spent their time on the swing-slide set.

We might continue to play outside in winter if the weather was warm enough. *Fox and Geese* was a tag game, with a long history, that was played in new-fallen snow. It required tramping out a path in a wagon-wheel shape with at least four spokes going out from a round safe zone in the middle. The fox and geese were all expected to stay on the paths once they were established. The fox would run the paths trying to tag the geese. It was an invigorating way to keep warm.

In more inclement winter weather, it was better to play in the gym. Our most common activity there was a tag game called *pom-pom-pullaway.* Either end of the gym was a safe base—beyond the basketball boundaries under the baskets. The person who was *it* stood in the middle and called "Pom-pom-pullaway, come away or I'll pull you away!" Everyone would then run from one end of the gym to the other. Anyone who was tagged then became *it* along with the original person. The game continued until all the runners were tagged. Then it was time to do it all over again with someone else starting as *it*—until the teacher's bell summoned us back to the classroom.

The Young Citizens League—YCL

South Dakota led the way, with a few other states following, to organize a program in elementary schools called the Young Citizens League (YCL). Each school or room would have a YCL chapter. About once a month on a Friday afternoon, our school had its YCL meeting. Classmates were elected to offices: president, vice president, secretary, maybe even a treasurer. We learned parliamentary procedure. In our business meetings we could make decisions about things such as who would put up, take down, and fold the flag, or who would clean the erasers and blackboards. It was a way to take responsibilities, learn democratic processes, and practice decision-making.

Some YCL activities were interschool events. There was a rally day each spring. On a Saturday, all of the half dozen or so schools in our third of the county came to Okaton. In the morning we had academic contests for spelling and arithmetic. Blue, red, and white ribbons were given for first, second, and third place in each event—perhaps, everyone got a ribbon. Each grade had an oral spelling bee and a written spelling contest. All words were taken from the list in each grade's spelling workbook.

Each grade also had an arithmetic competition testing our mastery of the basic addition and multiplication tables. The lower grades worked on the addition combinations and the higher grades on multiplication. We were timed in reciting the answers to all of the single-digit pairs from 1 to 9—eighty-one in all. There were *1 and 1, 1 and 2*, etc. up to *9 and 9*—each pair was set as an arithmetic problem with a line under it. The combinations were hand copied onto a blackboard in random order, and the contestants didn't see the combinations until they were brought into the room one at a time with their faces away from the board. When turned, each student was timed as she/he called out the answers to the combinations. To save time we began with the top row going from left to right, and the next row right to left, etc. Time was docked for any error. Whoever answered fastest and most accurately was the winner. Participating in this competition each year focused on mastery of the basics. I don't think students were required to participate, but all were encouraged to.

After a lunch prepared by a church women's group, there were the athletic events. The various contests were not identical each year, but normally there were running high jump, running broad jump, standing broad jump, and racing. Often there was a sack race that had us jumping the course in a gunny sack, or a three-legged race in which a pair of contestants, each with one leg tied to the partner, raced against other pairs. Some years the boys had a rooster fight: standing on one leg while holding the other foot in his hands, each of the two contestants tried to keep upright while toppling the other.

Some years the boys and girls raced against each other and sometimes not. I was not particularly athletic, but I always liked it better when I didn't have to race against the girls. If I were competing with only boys, I could usually win. But when I had to race against my cousin Alice Mae, she beat me every time.

Other events of YCL were the county and state gatherings. The county convention was in Murdo on a Saturday. Pageantry such as candle-lighting ceremonies and performances by the various schools were features of the program. Mrs. Gilbert's "Drum Major Drill Team" was a highlight one year. I cannot remember how I was nominated or elected, but in the eighth grade, I became YCL county president and thus MC for the county convention.

Each year three students from the county were selected as delegates for the State YCL Convention, alternating boys one year and girls the next. The delegates went to Pierre with Mabel Eggers, our county superintendent of schools, and stayed in the St. Charles Hotel near the Capitol. Miss Eggers stayed in one room and the county delegates in the next room. We had meetings in the chamber of the State House of Representatives and sat in the chairs of the legislators. Both my brother Gene and I had our turns as delegates in our sixth-grade years.

One of the highlights of the convention the year I attended was to hear our South Dakota Poet Laureate Badger Clark, read some of his poetry. (Being the Cowboy Poet, he preferred to be called the *Poet Lariat*.) He was getting old when I saw him, and he died two years later, the year I graduated from eighth grade. Besides the chosen delegates, our Okaton School had an opportunity to present our drill team program at the state convention in 1953, Mrs. Gilbert's last year with us.

Yearly declamatory contests were one more YCL activity. In each grade of the local schools a student was chosen to represent his/her school. An elimination round was held in each of the county's three town schools. The winners went to the county contest, and county finalists, to the state. Some grades were assigned to read a poem from the *South Dakota State Poetry Book* used by each school. It had a section for each grade level. The contestants would not know which poem they would be asked to read until the day of the contest. Other grades prepared something of their own choosing.

One year, my sister and I both won our way to the state contest in Pierre. Crystal had prepared a story about two little Eskimo children. She used a flannelgraph board on an easel. Her paper characters, their igloo, and other items of her story had flannel on the back. The nap of the material made it possible to move things around the board to illustrate her story. That same year, I did a humorous dramatic reading—one that Dad had done himself years before—about a man addressing an audience in a humorous accent that I attempted to imitate.

After the county contest, I overheard a neighbor comment to Mom about her two children both going to the state contest. Surely it was meant as a compliment, but Mom responded, "We expect our children to do well." I was never quite sure how to understand that response.

One More Basketball Team

Okaton's last high school basketball team played the year before the high school closed—the 1949-50 school year, when two seventh graders were on the team.

The next Okaton basketball team, launched in 1956-57, was not a regular school program, and none of the players were in high school. Our neighbor and family friend, Russell Tedrow (the same man who saved us after my first driving attempt), had once imagined becoming a school coach. But he was making his living working on the railroad section—checking and repairing the tracks daily. When his two boys reached fifth and sixth grades, Mr. Tedrow decided it was time to organize an elementary basketball team.

The team he put together included his son Ronald, my brother Gene, and Elvis Crazy Bear, all in sixth grade; Douglas Tedrow, in fifth; Johnny Daum, in fourth; and me, in eighth. We practiced many evenings in the

Okaton *crackerbox* until it was time to go to a tournament in Belvidere, which is in the next county west of Okaton on the Railroad and US Highway 16. We played teams from Belvidere, Wanblee on the Pine Ridge Reservation, and perhaps some schools I have forgotten.

Our coach told us when to play and when to sit on the bench. I was the oldest and tallest player, but not the best. I was disappointed not to get to play much of the time. (This was an omen of my high school experiences to come: I never made it onto any basketball team, not even the freshman team or the junior varsity my sophomore year.) But I was not the only one disappointed at the tournament in Belvidere. Years later my sister Crystal reminded me that she had practiced with the boys in Okaton but was then told she couldn't play in the tournament. Always resourceful, she decided to be our cheerleader.

Despite all our practice, we had the same problem the high school team before us had: we had practiced in our *crackerbox* with eight and a half foot baskets. As I remember, we lost all our tournament games. But it was a good experience, nevertheless. Our team had the opportunity to interact with children of other schools that we had no previous relationship with. Perhaps that basketball experience helped my brother Gene, who did get to play on high school basketball teams a few years later.

Although Okaton School did not offer everything a larger school might, it offered a rounded and diverse education, a hardworking faculty, and a mostly consistent student body. It reflected the enthusiasm of the young State of South Dakota to invest in its youngest citizens. I am deeply grateful for the start I received.

As the Schools Closed and Consolidated

Several years after we left, Okaton the school closed, and a private citizen bought it. He has converted it to a family dwelling. It must be one of the most spacious and unusual homes in the area.

The smaller one-room schools in the area have either been torn down or put to other uses. The small Grandview school was built about 1910. It was where Mrs. Martin had taught before coming to Okaton. Years after it was closed, the building was moved five miles from its place next to what had been the van Rooyen home, to a farm east of Okaton. In 2023 it is being retrofitted as the Grandview Art Gallery by Cristen Joy Roghair, a prolific photographer, and her rancher husband Marty, the son of my cousin Melvin. They live on the farm where the school is now. Okaton residents have good ideas of how to make use of what is available to them.

TWENTY-ONE

Prairie Ranchers 4-H Club

A new opportunity came in the fall of 1953 as I was starting fourth grade. Our neighbors, Bill and Mabel Graham, were ranchers living on the floodplain of the White River with hay and pastureland on the flat terrain and on the bluffs rising from the river. They invited families with children about the age of Gene and me and a little older to their home to discuss starting a 4-H club. The Grahams weren't in our school district, but they were on our party phone line, as were several other families who attended. We represented at least four small school districts—about ten or fifteen youth, ready to start our club.

The 4-H clubs across the country were, and still are, a part of the work of the US Department of Agriculture through the Cooperative Extension Service of each state's Land Grant Agricultural College. Jones County's Extension service related to South Dakota State College at Brookings (now South Dakota State University) and supported both 4-H clubs and Women's Home Extension Clubs.

The four *H*'s in the name of the clubs for youth are spelled out in the often-repeated motto: "I pledge my *head* to clearer thinking, my *heart* to greater loyalty, my *hands* to larger service, and my *health* to better living,

145

for my club, my community, my country, and my world." Being 4-H'ers prepared us to pursue many areas of interest.

The families that came together to organize our 4-H club were a mix of "cattle ranchers" and "dirt farmers." Our situation was a little like the song from the musical "Oklahoma" declaring: "The Farmers and the Cowmen should be friends." We *were* friends, but there was a clear distinction. When we started to discuss the name of our new club, people began throwing out suggestions. I always liked working with words and joined the discussion with a suggestion that sounded good to me. "Prairie Ranchers," I said. No sooner had those words come out of my mouth, than I heard a grunt or gasp from my dad. He didn't say anything aloud, and I don't know if anyone else noticed. His son's suggestion was accepted. I had just named the new club *Prairie Ranchers*. But we were *farmers*.

Over the years I have thought about the club's name and my dad's reaction. Was he shocked that we had picked a name that put the club on the one side of an invisible divide? Was he disappointed in me for proposing it? I never talked to him about that, and he never mentioned it. So, I was left to wonder. But Dad was a good sport. He and Mom actively supported our participation in 4-H, an activity that made it possible for us to gain exceptional skills and confidence. Gene and I immediately became members, and Crystal joined when she got a little older.

Indeed, the major projects for our club were Beef and Range Management. Every year, each member raised a calf to show. I don't think there was any member who didn't have at least one animal. Although we were farmers, Dad always had a dozen or so cows in his herd. They were not of high-quality breeding stock. Besides that, they were always off schedule from all the neighbors' cattle. We boarded the bull of a neighbor after his own cows had been bred, and he didn't want the bull around. So our cows had their calves in the fall, while everyone else's came in the spring, and any calves Gene and I got from Dad were always in an age class by themselves. Since they were not from quality breeding stock, they didn't receive blue ribbons.

Like many counties across the country, Jones County had had its own county fair. But before our 4-H club was formed, the fairs had been discontinued when civic leaders in Murdo found it too much of a burden to launch the expected grand celebration. With the demise of the Jones County Fair, local 4-H leaders developed county Achievement Days, an alternate opportunity for members to compete and share their work—without the rides and grandstand shows expected at fairs.

The 4-H Achievement Days featured a four-level award system for each competition, with everyone getting a ribbon. White was third place, a recognition of participation. Projects judged to be of better quality got a red second place ribbon, or a blue first. Each of these levels might be awarded to more than one competitor. A single top entry in each competition received a purple ribbon and was eligible to go on to the South Dakota State Fair in Huron or, for livestock, to the Western Stock Show in Rapid City.

Our club members were all in Beef and Range Management Projects. Besides raising animals, we studied the weeds and grasses on the range land. Each year we were required to collect a different selection of local plants, dry them, and put them in a specimen book. Collecting native grasses, the first year was easy, but in the following years we progressed through multiple types of weeds. The year we were collecting poisonous weeds, larkspur was on our list. Luckily for the cattle it had never appeared in our pastures or hay fields, so our leader Mabel Graham assisted us by ordering a package of larkspur seeds from a flower catalogue. She grew the beautiful, but poisonous, larkspur plants in her vegetable garden, enabling all of us to add them to that year's specimen books.

Gene and I were part of the 4-H club for four years. I still have my record book that reminds me we were each awarded special calves. One year, Gene successfully caught a calf in an Achievement Day calf-catching event. He brought it home to raise. Another year, I was one of several 4-H members in the county to be awarded a breeding heifer. She had been donated by a rancher or businessman and granted to me on the basis of points accumulated by my various exhibits judged at that Achievement Day. I got a blue ribbon for that heifer the following year.

When our sister, Crystal, joined the club, she received a special calf in her first year. Johnnie Daum, one of our church members, took a fancy to Crystal and gave her a black Angus calf. The calf stood out because most, if not all, of the other calves being shown were white-faced Herefords. She and her beautiful black calf did well at the next Achievement Day.

It wasn't until my fourth year in 4-H that I was able to enroll in a crop project which involved growing ten acres of wheat. Perhaps it was a relief to Dad for me to finally take on something in 4-H specific to farming. He had likely foreseen the predominant emphasis of ranch over farm projects when we started, and I had so casually named our club. My summer that year was spent driving the tractor for Dad, and he gave me a 10-acre field of wheat as pay for the summer. My crop sold for about $800.

Each year I was in Prairie Ranchers I exhibited several handicraft items. I made articles of wood, copper, aluminum, and tooled leather including belts, purses, and a ring binder. I did projects in electricity, vegetable gardening and tractor maintenance. We practiced public speaking by preparing talks and demonstrations for our meetings. Given such a full range of areas to learn about, practice in, report on, and compete in, none of us could be involved in anything every year. We certainly did keep busy and learned plenty.

My first year in 4-H, I jumped right into doing demonstrations. The format was a fifteen or twenty-minute presentation, showing how to do something. When I was just a fourth grader, I followed directions I had read and made a "handy feed scoop," and then I prepared a demonstration.

I showed my audience how to take a five-quart Havoline oil can, discarded by a gas station in Murdo, and cut off a half-moon shaped piece from the side of the can, leaving the vertical seam on the short side. I then bent over the sharp edge made by the cut, punched four holes into the seam on the short edge, and placed bolts through the holes to attach a four-inch steel handle. Presto: a "handy feed scoop!"

Mom was especially helpful in teaching me how to make the presentation with detailed posters outlining the project. We didn't have magic markers, so I meticulously cut individual letters from construction paper and pasted them onto white posterboard. It was a time-consuming project, but the results were worth it. I first gave my demonstration of making a feed scoop for a monthly club meeting. The club leaders encouraged me to do it at a county elimination round, and after I passed that, I gave it again for the county Achievement Day. I won a purple ribbon and was bound for the State Fair in Huron in September, just as I was starting fifth grade. My presentation at the State Fair gained me a white ribbon. I was excited to be competing there with older kids, some even in high school. In Jones County the older age group hadn't been as motivated as I was to do demonstrations, so I hadn't faced such strong competition as I had at the State Fair. I think I made enough handy feed scoops that year to last a lifetime!

Having gone to the State Fair with a demonstration, I was not eligible to compete with another the following year. But I developed a demonstration when I was again eligible. By then, I was doing a 4-H tractor maintenance project. My demonstration that year was cleaning a carburetor. I am not sure how many hours or days our Minneapolis Moline model U tractor was out of service because I had its carburetor off. But, on or off, it was always clean! I took that demonstration to the State Fair and received a blue ribbon. I don't know how many blues were awarded, but I was happy to get one. Learning to give demonstrations was a great opportunity for me. I honed public speaking and presentation skills that have served me well throughout my life.

My family came to Huron to see me give my first State Fair demonstration on the feed scoop. Mom had aunts, uncles, and cousins she liked to visit in the Huron area, some of whom had commercial stands at the Fair. When I was starting seventh grade, I don't think my family accompanied me to watch me clean a carburetor. Perhaps I rode to Huron with Joy Paine who worked for the State Extension Service in Jones County.

The monthly meetings of our 4-H club opened with singing led by one of the members. We had an elected president to preside, a vice president, and a secretary to take minutes. I filled several offices and sometimes led singing. Individual members took assignments to give brief talks on health or safety issues, or demonstrations in any number of areas. Our club was small enough that we all knew one another well, so we could feel comfortable among our friends as we gained competence.

The opportunities to prepare, exhibit, and compete at the county Achievement Days provided the year's most intensive 4-H activities. But throughout the year there were county events including an awards night and several social nights just for fun. They were usually held in the community hall in Draper with time for square and circle dancing. My brother Gene and I were stimulated in our pre-adolescent years by these folk dancing interactions and came home with our list of girls we called our "girlfriends." The girls had no knowledge of being on our lists. Maybe we had just seen them from a distance, or maybe we had asked one of them to be a dance partner. Occasionally the girls were asked to choose boys as partners. It was a great way to begin to learn the ways of social interaction.

An unexpected consequence of our involvement in 4-H was that Gene and I developed our own language. It was to enable us to privately discuss our listed 4-H girls. We pronounced English words backwards. Diphthongs like *th* or *sh* were challenging, but we kept the familiar sounds.

150

We called our language *Eneg dna Semaj* from our own names. We got quite proficient at it but kept it to ourselves. Crystal was a bit young to understand what we were doing—although she may have understood more than we thought. Wally was a toddler, not ready for such tricks, and I don't think our parents wanted to be bothered with our language. It was ours alone, and we still remember some of it. We eventually lost touch with most of the girls who were on our lists.

State 4-H Camps were held in the Black Hills each summer. Clubs from three or four counties of the State would be grouped for three-day camping experiences—not always the same groupings each year. A number of our club members always travelled together. Once, instead of going in several cars, our transportation to camp was in the back of a farm truck with a tarp over us as we sat on hay bales for the three-hour trip. It may not have been luxurious, but it was memorable and fun.

Just after I had graduated from eighth grade, I attended my final 4-H camp. There I met Judy, a girl about my age from Bennett County. In our brief time, we ate meals, played volleyball, and walked from place to place together. For those few days we were an item—perhaps boy and girlfriend. Other kids said that Judy and I should be voted the Queen and King of camp the following year. Nothing came of that, because our family moved out of state, and Judy and I went our own ways. I saw her only once several years later when we were in South Dakota for a family reunion, and later she sent me a letter to let me know she was getting married.

Along with our school and church, I rank 4-H as a top source of my learning and personal development.

Jim Roghair, age 12, giving a demonstration "Making
a Handy Feed Scoop," at the South Dakota State
Fair, Huron South Dakota, September 1955.

TWENTY-TWO

Always an Educational Opportunity

Although our family lived in a rather isolated rural environment, our parents always encouraged broad interests. Our childhood experiences became ongoing educational opportunities.

Sense of Direction

We lived on land that had been carefully surveyed with boundaries laid out in one mile and even half-mile square plots. Mile lines were usually visible, marked by fences and often by unmaintained private roads or established dirt township or county roads. We learned to recognize the miles lines and the compass directions early. I can't remember a time when I didn't know what was west or south, and it was expected that visitors, too, would know and understand. They would be instructed to go so many miles east and then so many miles north—nothing about turning to the right or left.

At an early age we also learned to read maps. A great learning tool to enhance that skill was a map of South Dakota tacked to the kitchen wall near our dining table for ready reference. That map had the customary orientation, west to the left and east to the right, etc. But our kitchen map hung on an east wall. So as I stood looking at it, I associated the west to the left of the map with what was actually on my left, the real north. The reality of the true compass directions that I knew well in our community became confused in my mind with the symbolic view of the map on the wall. As we anticipated a trip, especially one of the long trips to Oregon, I imagined our going in a real northerly direction (left on our kitchen map) rather than to the actual west which was behind me as I looked at the map. Of course, the imagined direction became an anticipation, and often when I got to a new place my inner sense of direction was a quarter turn off.

As a result, throughout my life, the imagined orientation of a map and the inner sense of the real geographical orientation have often been confused in my mind. I am always happy when I get to a new area and find out that my sense of direction in that place seems to correspond to what I think of as *South Dakota directions* rather than *map directions*. (Of course, in the mountainous area where I live in retirement, going home from Santa Fe, I drive a northbound highway headed toward Denver, but I actually travel a number of miles almost directly south to get around a mountain. More directional mind games!)

Long Trips

Because my mother's parents, brothers, and all but one sister had moved from South Dakota to Oregon during World War II, we usually took a trip to the West Coast to visit them every other year. We would leave after the wheat was planted in September and plan to be home long before the winter snowstorms would begin. As we travelled by car—a 1939 Ford, later a 1949 model, and finally a 1957—it would be about a three-day trip in each direction. Taking advantage of various travel routes, Dad always planned stops that were interesting and educational—historical landmarks, parks, or museums. In the states we crossed, we stopped at several commemorations of the Lewis and Clark expedition. We kept encountering references to their Native guide Sacajawea. We saw her mentioned so often that we kids got the impression she had been everywhere. Maybe she had!

Not only did we learn about geography and history on our trips, we also studied. We took our schoolbooks, so we didn't get behind during our two or three weeks of absence in September or October. When I was in first grade, Mom worked with me in the car on my reading and other subjects. I was surprised to discover that I was ahead of the other kids in my class when we got home. Ordinarily we did not have homework, but when we travelled, Mom made sure we kept up.

On our biennial trips to the West Coast, we stayed in inexpensive motels along the highway—many of them in the broad expanse of Montana. We never had advance reservations, and our parents often inspected the room before they registered.

In Oregon we visited grandparents, aunts, uncles, and cousins. Some relatives took us on excursions into the Cascade Mountains or to the Pacific Ocean—both novel to prairie kids. One year our trip was expanded into Washington State where we visited members of Mom's extended family and rode across Puget Sound on two large ferry boats, one of which was the famed Kalakala. I clearly remember a dark night when Dad took me up to the wheelhouse of one ferry to see the captain steering the boat with the vast array of dials he was using to navigate. I was small, and to get up there, Dad cradled me in one arm while he held onto an outside ladder with the other hand. The deep water churned below us.

On another trip we went through the Sequoia forests in California and visited more of Mom's relatives. Once, while we were staying in Salem, Oregon, we took a quick trip across the Coast Range to Tillamook, Oregon, and visited people Dad had known in Okaton. We observed the varied landscapes, geography, and cultures on those long family trips.

Learning at Home

Of course, we didn't have to leave home for family education. Besides the daily kitchen-table Bible readings, we heard Greek, Roman, and Norse myths or other stories and poems from a thick children's literature textbook Mom had kept from college. One of the poems in the book Dad especially liked to read was "The Deacon's Masterpiece: or the Wonderful 'One Hoss Shay'; A Logical Story" by Oliver Wendell Holmes. The shay (chaise or carriage) was built in such a wonderful way that no part of it ever wore out until after one hundred years ". . . it went to pieces all at once, and nothing first—just as bubbles do when they burst." Living with things that had to be constantly repaired, Dad appreciated and shared with us the absurdity of a perfection that would finally burst like a bubble.

Our home education was not limited to listening to stories read to us. Sitting around the meal table was required, from the opening blessing before the meal to the closing prayer of thanksgiving. But we *were* permitted to go into the living room and bring back to the table Mom's *Merriam Webster Collegiate Dictionary* when a question about the meaning or spelling of a word came up. It was a necessary and permitted distraction from the meal.

Learning about Music

We always had an old upright piano, and Mom enjoyed playing it. She could read music and sometimes did, especially popular sheet music. But she most enjoyed playing by ear the tunes she already knew. Dad could not read music or even carry a tune, but he liked music anyway. When each of us children were old enough, we had the opportunity to take music lessons if we wished. Mrs. Skinrood was a retired teacher in Okaton whose husband was not well; he was probably suffering from dementia. She gave piano lessons to children, and charged maybe fifty cents. I took piano lessons from her for a year or two starting when I was about six. I learned to read music and gained some piano fundamentals, but I never got very proficient. For several years after I quit the lessons, I would sit down at the piano now and then to slowly pick out a tune such as "America the Beautiful," but then not touch the instrument again for months. Crystal took piano lessons later from a woman in Murdo, and got fairly good at it, but the rest of the family claimed that she liked to speed up the music too much. I don't remember that Gene or Wally had any piano lessons, although they both took up the tuba in high school.

When I was about eight, a traveling salesman came to our farm home offering music lessons for kids: accordion, Spanish guitar, or Hawaiian guitar. I was interested, and although I don't think I had ever seen a Hawaiian (steel) guitar before, I was signed up for it. Purchase of a student guitar was part of the deal. The lessons were taught, first in a church in Murdo and later in a motel room. I enjoyed learning to play and practiced often while I was taking the lessons. I played and accompanied myself, and sometimes my siblings, while singing for church, community, and school events. As the lessons were coming to an end, there was an opportunity to buy an electric steel guitar that was to carry me to musical heights. The salespeople let us bring the instrument home, but by then, my interest had flagged. The new guitar sat in the living room for weeks, and I don't think I ever took it out of its case. Finally, my parents returned it, and that chapter ended without discussion.

John Deere Day

Going to John Deere Day was always a reason for Gene and me to miss school, and we both remember those experiences as highly educational. I don't think Crystal ever came to any of those shows—it appears that it was only during Dad and Mom's courtship that Dad took a woman or girl to the show. Wally was still quite small when we moved, so he likely missed John Deere Day altogether.

My cousin Cornelia who was about the same age as my brother Wally, and not yet in school when we moved away, has memories of John Deere Day. Her dad, our Uncle Albert, took her out of school to go to the programs the way Dad had taken us. She still remembers being the only female present and her dad claiming her presence cleaned up the language of the men attending.

Essay Contest

When I was in the seventh grade, my mother encouraged me to write an essay for a state contest on why I admired my friends who did not use alcohol and tobacco. I worked hard on the writing, and Mom, who loved to write, coached me. My piece won the one hundred-dollar first prize in the state. It was really the beginning of a life and career of writing.

Civics Lessons

The fall I was in eighth grade, Dad took me to meet George McGovern at a political campaign event in the Jones County Courthouse in Murdo. McGovern was the son of a Methodist minister from Mitchell, a town east of the Missouri River on the same railroad and highway as Okaton. He was running for the first time to be one of South Dakota's two members of the US House of Representatives. He gave me a campaign button which I have cherished through the years as I followed him from a distance. He later became a three-term US Senator and finally the Democratic candidate for President of the United States in 1972 but was defeated by Richard Nixon.

I met McGovern once again in the late 1990s when I sat next to him for lunch at the Union League in Chicago. He was there on a tour promoting his new book, *The Third Freedom: Ending Hunger in Our Time*. In my pocket I carried the campaign button he had given me in Murdo more than forty years earlier. He recognized the pin and identified it as from 1958.

I responded, "It couldn't have been that year, we had already moved to Oregon by then."

"Oh," he said, "then it was 1956; I used the same button both times." He remembered the campaign, but he did not recognized me as the youngster to whom he had given his pin.

Mother initiated an eighth-grade opportunity for me to interact with another politician who later became prominent. I took a day off from school for a field trip to the State Capitol in Pierre to see the legislature in action. Our newly elected state senator was Jim Abdnor, born in Kennebec and living in Presho, two towns east along Highway 16 in the next county. Abdnor agreed to welcome me and show me around the Capitol on the appointed day.

Dad's youngest sister Joanna, always known to the family as Joan (pronounced *Jo-Anne*) went with us to Pierre to be my chaperone while my parents did a little shopping. (Perhaps choosing Aunt Joan hinted at matchmaking; she and Abdnor, the new senator, were both single. If that was an intention, it had no results; he remained a bachelor his whole life. Eventually Aunt Joan married Bud Grover and had a good marriage living just outside of Rapid City.)

We spent the morning of my Capitol visit observing the State Senate. I have no recollection of what they were doing, and likely I didn't understand it. But when we went across the hall in the afternoon to see the House of Representatives in action, I got a totally different impression. It was February 14, 1957, and what I observed on the House floor was a Valentine's Day party. They were passing around cookies and candy, enjoying a break from their usual work. Aunt Joan and I observed it all from the gallery, but I don't remember any cookies being offered to us. It was an odd conclusion to the day on which I was supposed to learn how government works. Nevertheless, it was unforgettable.

Eventually Jim Abdnor, the son of an immigrant Lebanese farm family, made his way to the US House of Representatives, and later he defeated Senator McGovern for a seat in the US Senate as a Republican. I never suspected, as an eighth grader, that I was meeting in-person two Senators-to-be.

The Value of Education

Education was a high priority for our family. After our move to Oregon, Dad finally received his GED high school diploma in the same year I graduated from high school. While he was studying for the test, Mom suggested I help him with algebra, since I was doing well in my second year of it. But before I could explain any problem to him, I would discover that he had already reached the answer in his head. For years he had mentally calculated acres of farmland or the amount of seed needed for a field, so algebra came naturally to him.

In 1969, the year I graduated from Seminary, Mom finished her BA degree in education at Linfield College which was across the street from their McMinnville home. It was easy for her to afford the tuition since it was reduced or free because Dad was employed by the college as a maintenance electrician. Although her fellow students were all much younger than her, she was proud to have accomplished this milestone at the age of fifty-two.

Together, despite their own delayed educations, Mom and Dad produced a family who have earned multiple master's degrees and doctorates. My sister Crystal even became a town mayor. More master's degrees and doctorates have been awarded or are still in process for their grandchildren. Against the odds, our parents set us on a good path of continued learning which continues through the generations.

PART D
Siblings

PART II

Siblings

TWENTY-THREE

Brothers

When Mom and Dad brought Gene home from the hospital in February 1945, my first interaction with him was to bite him on the cheek—surely, I had been invited to give him a kiss. Although this was his introduction to life as a second child, we didn't become enemies. Actually, it wasn't long before Gene and I became partners in much that we did. One of the most serious early events between us occurred during the summer when I was four and he was two. We were both big enough to be out of the house and around the farm without constant parental oversight—helicopter parenting became popular a generation later. There were many opportunities to get into mischief on the farm, and we went about discovering them.

Every summer we had a big population of flies. To combat the insects, hand-held fly-sprayers were the most available weapon. By pulling out the handle and then pushing it back, one could deliver a heavy mist of DDT onto a cow's back before she was milked, or around the back door of the house before it was opened. Flies were everywhere, and so was DDT. I had not been entrusted to use DDT, but it was accessible, and the sprayer wasn't hard to use. In playful experimentation, I asked, "Gene, do you want me to spray you in the face?"

I clearly remember that he said "Yes," and I sprayed DDT in my brother's eyes.

With the poison stinging him, Gene ran crying into the house. Mom thoroughly washed his face and scolded me for what I had done. Gene did not retaliate, and, as far as I know, there were no long-term ill effects from the spray. It was something I inflicted on him, without malicious intent. I thought of him as my two-year-old co-conspirator—a fellow innocent experimenter. Of course, we were both too young to understand what we were doing. Like our community, we didn't even recognize DDT to be something dangerous. Sprayers full of the insecticide were simply among the hazards of growing up in the mid-1940s where we lived. And having a brother two years older was a hazard Gene had no choice but to live with.

Opportunities for trouble abounded. Years later, when we were in third and first grades respectively, we were waiting for Dad to pick us up after school. The teacher was still in the classroom, but we were outside "tearing around," as my mother would say—working off the pent-up energy from long hours of sitting at our desks. Near the back door of the school were coal cinders and other trash that had been tossed into the furnace and then discarded onto the ground. (Likely all the kids in school got skinned knees from falling on the debris.) Waiting for Dad, Gene and I started throwing junk at one another. I picked up a broken ink bottle. I didn't usually have a very good aim and rarely hit anything, but that day I hit Gene in the forehead with the glass. He began to bleed. I helped him back into the school, and the teacher applied first aid before Dad arrived. It was an injury simply treated at home, but Gene still has a scar on his forehead. I was old enough to know better than to throw a broken bottle at my little brother, so Mom disciplined me with a spanking using her favorite tool, a wooden spoon. Dad didn't say much.

There was another incident at school which blurs in my memory with that of the ink bottle, but for which I have felt a bit more guilt.

Gene, however, remembers it more clearly than I and is sure that it was an accident. We were never supervised during recesses, and usually the whole school of fifteen or so kids played together. Often, we played cops and robbers. Divided more or less equally into two teams, it was the job of the cops to capture the robbers and place them in the jail, located on the concrete steps leading down to the furnace room. Other robbers could come and tag their captured teammates to get them out of jail.

Gene was reaching through the pipe railing just above ground level, trying to tag one of the robbers a few feet down. On the same team, I was holding one of Gene's arms while he tried to reach the child below. It was a dangerous maneuver, and I lost my grip. Gene tumbled down onto a steel barrel that sat in our jail. He sustained a serious gash to the back of his head.

I helped Gene back into the school, and the teacher applied cloths to stop the bleeding. School work for the day was abandoned. I have no idea who got the word to our parents, but shortly, Dad came to the school. It was obvious that the cut required medical attention, so Dad took Gene for emergency help. He dropped me off at my Grandma Roghair's house on the way and drove ten miles east to Murdo, where he planned to have the county's only doctor attend to Gene.

Our parents didn't like that doctor, and we usually went to one in the next county. People said the local doctor spent too much time in the pool hall—the only place in town that sold alcohol. But Gene's condition was urgent, and Dad sought the nearest help, in spite of his distrust of the doctor. Dad's concerns were justified that afternoon; the doctor *was* in the pool hall, and he seemed *not* up to his professional oath. He responded to the emergency by asking, "Aren't you one of Dr. Sundet's patients? Take him to Dr. Sundet." That sent Dad and Gene, not only the ten miles back to Okaton, but another thirty-five or more miles west to Kadoka, the next county seat. They found Dr. Sundet, and Gene was ultimately stitched up properly, with only a permanent scar to mark the event.

Dad didn't express his anger often, but the behavior of the doctor in Murdo enraged him. When he got home, Dad threatened to complain to the American Medical Association, and I think he really intended to do it. But it was an unfulfilled threat. Instead, the incident became a story Dad told over and over for years, and always with the addendum: "I should have. . ." The AMA never got Dad's complaint, and the doctor continued to practice in Murdo for several more years.

I don't remember Gene's inflicting injury on me, but he recalls hitting me on the head with a bottle at our home. It was what little boys did to each other, especially when parents weren't looking. As we matured, I learned to take a more cautious approach to Gene. While we were still quite small, people used to see us together, and ask, "Are they twins?" Gene grew much faster than I did. During our grade school years, he and I could usually wear the same clothes. Gene also grew stronger and more athletic. By the time I started high school at the age of fourteen, I had reached my mature height of five feet ten and a half inches. At that time Gene was twelve, but he kept growing until he eventually reached six feet three inches.

By the time he was my size, I stopped picking physical fights with him, although I occasionally enticed him to hold out his arm to test our arm lengths. That was one contest I could always win. My arms were longer, and I could poke his underarm, but he couldn't reach mine. He disliked it, but I did try it many times, anyway. Having longer arms was my only physical advantage over Gene.

In spite of intermittent trauma at each other's hands, Gene and I were really best friends and cooperated on many things. Shortly after the REA electric service came to our home in 1952, when I was nine, we pooled our money for a major purchase. From the Sears Roebuck or Montgomery Ward catalogue we ordered a Marx electric toy train set. Gene remembers the cost to be $14.98—just a little cheaper than the Lionel we might have gotten. It came by mail, packed in a sturdy cardboard box with many postage stamps on it. In this container it would be stored for many years, with each piece having its own resting spot.

Since our house was small, there was no place for the train and track to remain assembled. Each time we played with them, we had to remove every piece from its compartment in the box. The three-rail track was assembled in its oval pattern. The transformer was plugged into a wall outlet, and its wires were attached to the track. We carefully set the 4-6-4 model steam engine on the track, coupled with its coal tender, a box car, a tank car, a coal car, and a caboose. With the control on the transformer, we started the train, regulated its speed, stopped it, and reversed its direction. Gene and I were proud to watch our little train go around and around its track. We didn't know anyone else who had a train, and it was a special occasion whenever the train resumed its place in the middle of the linoleum living room floor. Sometimes we got it out for guests. In time we added three streamlined passenger cars to the freight train. Nothing was lacking.

Our train purchase was made with money we had earned by selling farm produce to a neighbor in town. Neither of us remembers exactly what we sold or to whom. Perhaps it was a domestic duck that lived on our dam, or duck eggs that were larger and richer than chicken eggs. Sometimes our cow produced more milk than we could use, and we sold a gallon—unpasteurized and whole.

We bought the train the year before a larger economic adventure began—the day Dad brought home two pigs for us to raise. Gene and I kept them in a small pen in the barn and fed them scraps and slop from the house, as well as grain from our farm. Eventually the time came to sell them. We didn't get rich from the sale, but we put a few dollars into our savings accounts at the Okaton State Bank. Because they had been raised like pets, appropriately, Dad didn't butcher either of these animals for our consumption.

Living on the farm, Dad always had two single shot guns in the house: a .22 caliber rifle and a 12-gauge shotgun. Neither was used very often, and they did not have an important place in our family life. Dad was not a hunter, but guns were a part of normal home equipment. Dad kept some shotgun shells loaded with wheat grains, rather than lead, that he used to chase away unwanted dogs or cattle that might wander onto our property. Occasionally Mom might try to get him to use the shotgun to get a grouse for us to eat, but I don't remember ever having such a meal. Most often, if we used either gun at all, it was the .22 with short rifle bullets for target practice.

Gene and I took gun safety training from the National Rifle Association. The training was a simple course on safe gun use; the NRA had not yet morphed into a national political organization. Our classes were held in the county courthouse in Murdo. After we took the course, our parents allowed us to get a Daisy BB gun. It was a way to learn a little about guns without high risk. Gene liked to use it to shoot sparrows that lived in the rafters of our barn. I was never sure why we should shoot birds, but it was something boys did in those days. I did not use the BB gun very much and can't remember ever shooting any living thing.

It must have been Gene's idea, but after the BB gun, I agreed with him that we should have a better gun. We collaborated to purchase from a catalogue a .22 caliber air rifle. It was a real gun, but instead of gunpowder propelling the lead bullets, they were powered by compressed air. The gun had to be physically pumped many times before each shot—if I remember correctly, it took about twenty pumps.

Gene and I got good exercise hunting rabbits while walking across the expanse of open prairie, the tilled fields of summer fallow, or the wheat stubble. We each carried a single-shot rifle; one of us had our new air rifle, and the other, Dad's rifle, loaded with .22 long rifle bullets with a one-mile range. Either gun we used meant stopping to reload after each shot—pumping the air rifle extensively or reloading Dad's gun. Since the rabbits always kept a safe distance, and our aim was not exceptional, there was plenty of time for our prey to increase the space between us and them. We didn't offer much danger to either of the two species of rabbit we pursued, the cottontails with the small ears and fluffy tails or the jackrabbits (really hares) with long ears. We hoped to have rabbit stew sometime, but we never brought anything home. Nevertheless, we brothers enjoyed sharing our collaborative hunting trips.

Gene has always been much more of an outdoorsman than I. As a pre-adolescent he trapped muskrats, skinned them, and sold the pelts. Thus, he performed the important role of keeping the rodents from penetrating the earthen bank and draining the water out of our dam. He enjoyed that activity, but it was not an interest we shared.

When we left the farm, Gene went on to be a junior high and high school athlete in basketball and football, the two major sports of our schools in Oregon. I tried out for many teams, but never got on one, except for track. On that team the coach let me run some races but seemed to appreciate my score-keeping more than my running; Gene was our family athlete.

After our early days of tormenting each other were over, we came to appreciate the gift of being brothers. Our rich childhood experiences shaped who we would each become. When he was nineteen years old, Gene spent a summer hitchhiking from the US West Coast to the East and back again, earning his livelihood as he went. Gene told me, "The trip took me to Washington, Arizona, Texas, Florida, D.C., New York, Michigan, and back to Oregon with all the intervening states." It even included some farm work for family members in South Dakota.

In his twenties, he spent several years in India among poor villagers working with the Peace Corps and later as a scholar of an Indian language. He returned to India several times, earning a PhD in the Telegu language from the University of Wisconsin. His project consisted of field recording of Telugu oral epics, and the translation and publication of one extended version of over thirty hours. These epics are still performed by traveling troupes. His ground-breaking thesis was published by Oxford University Press. Other work included collaboration on the translation of a thirteenth century Telugu Saivite text.

In addition to India, he traveled to Nepal and other exotic places. He has done a limited amount of teaching and some translating from Telegu but has made most of his living in sales. Gene is the most rugged, adventurous, and independent one in our family, characteristics that began developing when he was very young.

Sometimes I wonder how much Gene's early experiences of being the second child helped shape him into the adventurer he would become. Was I unintentionally a part of his survival training and the development of his adventurous approach to life?

Gene and Jim with cucumbers from our garden.

TWENTY-FOUR

The Arrival of a Sister

When my sister Elaine Crystal Roghair was born in July 1947, I was four and a half years old, to the day. Whereas my birth in January 1943 gave me an extraordinarily cold start, hers was during a July heat wave. The daily high temperature was near 100° for many days. We had no electricity or air conditioning on the farm, even the hospital in the city had no air conditioning.

Grandma Crystal Bowder came by train, halfway across the country from Salem, Oregon, to stay with Dad, Gene, and me while Mom was in Pierre waiting. Fathers were not expected to be a part of the birth experience in those days, and the mid-summer farm work was keeping Dad busy. Besides the daily chores of feeding chickens and milking our cow, there was the preparation of the harvest machinery and the storage space for the still ripening winter wheat. Final tilling of the summer fallow before the September planting of next year's crop also continued. Farm work was never done, and Grandma's presence in our home made it possible for Dad to continue his work.

At the time of Crystal's birth, Gene was almost two and a half and needed more constant attention than I did. It seemed special to us to have our maternal grandma with us. We didn't know her as well as we did Grandma Roghair and the other members of Dad's family who lived in our community, but we welcomed her presence and learned much from her.

Mom was boarding in a private home in Pierre, South Dakota, near St. Mary's Hospital. It seemed to me she was gone a long time. We wondered why it was so long. I now understand that it was due to the distance and the condition of the highways that mothers-to-be stayed in Pierre.

Before I was born, all of our family had been born at home, with local midwives. My cousin Alice and I began a new family tradition by being born in a hospital. In 1943 it was in Chamberlain where Aunt Harriet was working. But by the mid-1940s our aunt had moved to a more distant place, and our family began using the hospital in Pierre, only about seventy-five miles from our home.

We were familiar with Pierre, since we went there as a family at least two or three times a year to patronize the J.C. Penney store and other smaller shops to buy such things as winter parkas and footwear. But the trip to Pierre always seemed a considerable distance on the roads of 1947. Of course, the first mile and a half from our farm was dirt with no gravel, only gumbo—impassable by car after a summer rain—and no one in our area had a four-wheel drive vehicle yet. The next thirty miles were on the original US 16, a major national east-west highway, but still a narrow blacktop, two-lane highway passing through the center of three small towns. Traveling the last forty miles on north-south US 83 was more desolate, with no towns and a narrower highway. At least it was blacktopped, in contrast to the long stretch of 83 that was still gravel going south of Murdo to the Nebraska border.

The closer the road came to Piere, the steeper the hills. It seemed almost mountainous as it entered the Missouri River breaks and finally the floodplain. Fort Pierre, on the west bank, was one of the original

Missouri River towns. A suspension bridge took us across to the capital, Pierre, a slightly larger town. On a good day it took several hours to get to Pierre from our home, but when it rained, we couldn't even get out of our driveway. It was later in 1947 that Dad purchased the four-wheel-drive Willys Jeep. It may be hard to imagine facing those conditions now—with the improved highways, people can drive to Pierre in about an hour.

Grandma Bowder was a great help to our family. She kept us fed, clean, happy, and out of the blazing sun to the extent that she could. Every morning we listened for news from Pierre, the radio voice we called *Mrs. Pierre*—really Ida McNeil. She and her husband Dana had started the radio station in their home in 1915. Dana had long since died, but Mrs. McNeil continued serving the broader community as a vital link for years to come. Every morning she read the list of people in the small hospital and gave a brief summary of their conditions—mostly "resting well." Such a valuable service to the community would be unthinkable with more current HIPPA privacy rules. But it would be about twenty years before reliable telephone service was available on the farms, so the radio service was vital.

The announcement we were listening for was, "A baby girl born to Mr. and Mrs. Ed Roghair." We heard it along with everyone who had tuned in that Thursday morning. Our sister had been born the day before. Since children were not welcome as visitors in the hospital, while Dad and Grandma Bowder went to Pierre to visit Mom and the baby, Gene and I were left with Grandma Roghair. Several of our aunts and uncles were still living with her and Grandpa; they would all meet the new baby when she came home from the hospital.

Dad and Mom chose to name our sister Elaine Crystal, but to call her by her middle name, or the nickname Crysti. She was named after Grandma Bowder whose name was Cora Crystal but had always been called Crystal. For reasons unknown, Grandma and each of her siblings, male and female, were named after gemstones, Garnet, Opal, Pearl, etc. Now, she was proud to have a new granddaughter named after her. But Grandma Roghair always called her Sparkle! Could it be she was jealous? Grandma's nickname for our sister was never explained, but it always felt more positive than negative.

After a number of days in the hospital, according to common practice, Crysti and Mom came home. It was exciting to have a new sister enter our young lives. Grandma Bowder stayed a few more days, then we all went back to Pierre with her so she could catch the Chicago and North Western train to Oregon. A puffing steam locomotive pulled the passenger train. We didn't realize at the time that we were near the end of an era. By 1956 steam locomotives were replaced by modern diesel-electric engines that hauled the passenger cars until that service, too, was discontinued a few years later.

Life was not easy in those days. Proper sanitation was a goal, but not always achievable. Mother nursed Crysti as long as she could. The milk the rest of us drank was whole, un-pasteurized, and easily contaminated with flecks of barnyard dust. The new baby would have boiled milk when she started to use a bottle. But we lived with outdoor toilets and shared our weekly bath water in a small square galvanized tub on the kitchen floor. Although our parents took all possible precautions for feeding and bathing the baby, Crysti became ill with whooping cough when she was just weeks old—too young to have been vaccinated. No one knew how she contracted it. I remember the seriousness—the hushed tones—as our parents worked to protect the baby's life. They took her to Doctor Kimball in Murdo, who had cared for the rest of us. I do not know what remedies he prescribed, and I was too young to grasp how seriously ill she really was. But in fact, Crysti nearly died, and her survival seems to have been a miracle.

As a little sister with two older brothers, she had advantages and disadvantages. Mom now had a little girl to dote on as any mother might.

Dad admired his daughter—he had always hoped to have a brown-eyed girl. Gene and I had a little one to play with and to learn to care for. But Gene and Crysti, just a little over two years apart, developed a hardy sibling rivalry that lasted for many years. Being a little older, I felt more protective of, than competitive with, my sister. I remember always having feelings of closeness and affection for her. But I did not consider my role the way Crysti described it years later; she said that I helped protect her from Gene. Perhaps that was true, but I did not realize it then.

When she was little, Crysti liked to sit in front of the mirror of Mom's vanity and primp herself. She liked to wear pretty dresses and to have her picture taken. But she was also ready to follow her dad and brothers around the farm and be involved in anything that was happening. Dad placed two tall wooden posts in the back yard to do double duty. They each held up the north end of two heavy wire clotheslines, and from a high brace between them he hung a rope swing with a wooden seat. The swing was put up at just the right time for Crysti, and swinging became a favorite pastime for her. Although we all enjoyed the swing, it became Crysti's domain.

When the 4-H club started, Gene and I immediately became members, but Crysti was too young to join. Eventually when Crysti was old enough to join, one of our church members, Johnnie Daum, wanted to do something special for her, and he gave her a well-bred Black Angus calf. Crysti was proud of her calf but did not put as much energy into training and showmanship as Gene and I did. We didn't think she and her calf would do well at the 4-H Achievement Day. But that day her calf followed Crysti's lead and did everything right. Together they got high honors for both showmanship and for the quality of the animal itself. Crysti was either much more skilled in showing the calf than we had thought, or really lucky.

Crysti was starting fifth grade in the Okaton School the fall we moved to McMinnville, Oregon. It always seemed to me that she quickly made many good friends in our new community. But she remembers it as a hard time—she missed our Okaton extended family and our hometown. The girls who had lived in McMinnville all of their lives were not ready to include newcomers. The new friends Crystal made were others who had recently arrived. They were also left out of the established cliques from several grade schools that had persisted into the single junior high and then high school.

As an adult, Crysti has led a healthy life, had a long marriage, and raised a son. Her successful and fruitful career has included time as a junior high drama teacher, a county planner, a chamber of commerce executive, a planning consultant, and three terms as Mayor of Coos Bay, Oregon. As a community leader she had much to do with the restoration of an old theater in her town and is a loyal volunteer in the local art museum.

She was a survivor from her earliest weeks, and became a strong woman, meeting and overcoming many of the hurdles that women her age have faced in business, community, and political realms. I am proud of my sister who has provided service and inspiration to our family and her community for many years.

Crystal at 16 months.

Crystal about 5 years old and Grandpa Bowder fishing.

TWENTY-FIVE

We Have a New Brother

My youngest brother Wallace Armand Roghair—Wally—born in May 1952, grew up in the same family as I did, but his childhood experiences were totally different from mine and those of my other siblings. He was never a pupil in the Okaton School and had no 4-H club experience. He did not learn much about raising animals, doing farm chores, or operating machinery. Five years old in the fall we left the farm, he started kindergarten in Oregon—the first in our family to attend any school before first grade. Of course, he had three older siblings to boss him around, care for him, or help him out. His was a different life.

Wally was born at a memorable time in the United States. I was nine and old enough to feel quite grown-up, but still young enough to be excited about the novelty of all that was happening in the world. Our nation was in its first Cold War conflict, the Korean War. Senator Joe McCarthy was finding communists behind every door. In the 1952 presidential election primary campaign my dad favored the man in the coonskin cap, the populist Democrat Senator Estes Kefauver of Tennessee. He won the New Hampshire primary, prompting the sitting President Harry Truman to withdraw. But the party convention chose Adlai Stevenson, who would eventually lose to Ike, General Dwight D. Eisenhower, the World War II hero. I wore both Kefauver and Stevenson buttons to school, but I also obtained an "I Like Ike" button. Everybody liked Ike, and probably no one could have beaten him that year.

Our local attention was on the reconstruction of US Highway 16, which would be replaced at Ike's initiative a few years later (after we moved) by Interstate 90. Despite the real disruption the road construction brought to the quiet life of Okaton, there were even bigger issues in 1952: the devastating winter storms and the flooding on the Missouri River that followed.

As the seasons of 1952 changed from winter to spring, Mom was in the late stages of her fourth pregnancy. For years, the backs of her legs had shown visible bluish varicose veins. She didn't complain of the pain they caused, but Mom might have been suffering in silence. As the pregnancy progressed, her legs became so painful that she had trouble getting around the house for ordinary activities. I don't think she had any medical attention for this condition, but I clearly remember the family's solution. Even at the times of her worst pain, Mom couldn't just stay in bed; she had a family to take care of. So, she was wheeled around the house on a *Babee Tenda* that had been purchased when Crysti was a baby.

This small, three-foot square table of wood and steel construction had a hard plastic tabletop. It stood a little higher than two feet, on sturdy steel legs with castors for easy movement around the house. In the center of the tabletop was a cutout just the right size to slip in a baby or toddler, who could sit in the seat hanging below the table surface with feet on a rest. Strapped in, a small child could be given food or other diversions and spend an extended time in the proximity of other family members while being held securely by this piece of furniture.

Mom's younger brother, our Uncle Clifford Bowder, was selling Babee Tendas at the time Crysti was born, and so Dad bought one for her. By 1952, Crysti was almost five and had long outgrown the Babee Tenda.

So the cover had been placed over the seat to make a small table. With an accompanying child's folding chair, this set was well-designed for the safety and comfort of a baby and for the use of a growing child. But its table was never meant as a transport for an adult. Nevertheless, we three older children remember pushing Mom around the house as she sat on the tabletop of the Babee Tenda, her painful legs dangling. Surely, she could have used a wheelchair, and undoubtedly, she deserved more medical advice and attention than she got. But the accommodation we remember is the Babee Tenda.

As the due date for Wally's birth drew near, the spring flooding in Pierre had peaked and begun to recede. Grandpa and Grandma Bowder drove nearly 1500 miles from Salem, Oregon, to our farm so Grandma could take over Mom's household duties. They arrived in Grandpa's green Buick, its passenger door safely tied shut by a piece of rope because of a faulty latch. Grandpa was always resourceful like that. I remember it as an old car, but likely it was not so old—surely it was a post-World War II model. Perhaps it had been in an accident or sustained rough use. Maybe Grandpa had acquired it from someone for whom he worked as a gardener, carpenter, or handyman; that was the way he acquired many things.

When Grandma arrived, she immediately took the pressure off Mom so she could rest her legs. Grandpa found other things to occupy and amuse himself. Gene and I remember one day when he took us fishing, and he offered us a drink of whiskey from a bottle he had under the car seat. We declined, as I'm sure he expected us to. But we never knew what to expect when Grandpa Bowder was around. He was always telling jokes and tall tales, and often Grandma would reprimand him with, "Oh, Frank!" But that didn't seem to alter his cadence very much.

As she did for the birth of each of her children, Mom stayed with a family near the hospital while awaiting her delivery. She was in Pierre and near the flooding Missouri River. The rest of us went about our lives and farm routines with Grandma's skilled assistance.

We still had no commercial phone line, and there were no national privacy guidelines. So again, we listened every morning for Mrs. Pierre's hospital report on KGFX radio. Finally, on a Sunday in May, it was announced that a baby boy had been born the night before to Mr. and Mrs. Ed Roghair of Okaton. Gathered around the breakfast table, we were excited when we heard the news: we had a new baby brother! We would not go to church that morning but would get in the car and drive to Pierre.

Crysti, almost five and quite capable of thinking for herself, was not so excited. She had previously expressed her preferences and now stated her disappointment: "I wanted a baby sister!" Regardless of Crysti's objections, we all went to Pierre, so Dad and Grandma could visit Mom and the baby boy.

Since no children could visit the hospital room, Gene, Crysti, and I played in Griffin Park, between St. Mary's Hospital and the Missouri River and on the historic Lewis and Clark Trail. Parts of the park were still flooded, but we found a place dry enough to spend our time while Dad and Grandma took turns visiting in the hospital and watching us in the park.

Our parents named our brother Wallace Armand, and eventually Mom and Wally came home. When Grandpa and Grandma went back to Oregon, life in our home settled into normal routines. But Gene and I—and even Crysti—had a new center of interest. Each of us began to take responsibilities within our capabilities to look after Wally. The attention he got was surely greater than any of us had received when we were his age. He became a sort of mascot for us older siblings.

When he was born, Wally had dark brown hair that was already over his ears. Dad commented, "He was born needing a haircut." We kids didn't cut his hair, but we loved to work with it. Putting Johnson's Baby Oil on his head and then brushing his hair up from both sides, we created a pointed ridge running from front to back. We called it his "swoop" hair style. We fixed his hair over and over until the novelty wore off. We loved to hold him, rock him, cuddle him. He was well-loved.

It was so much fun to have a baby brother that we didn't want to be away from him. Mom and her older sister, Aunt Frances, decided I should visit my aunt's family for a week in Aberdeen, South Dakota, to take swimming lessons. But Wally was only a few months old, and being away from the baby was my only objection to the trip. I didn't want to miss anything.

As Wally grew, we siblings were all involved in his learning and progress. I had him with me in the barn, showing him the animals, when Wally spoke his first recognizable word, "pig." It was a milestone for all of us.

We always had farm cats that lived in the barn or wherever they wished. They got a little food from us, particularly a shot of milk squirted in their direction while one of us was milking the cow. But mainly they fended for themselves. They were supposed to keep down the mouse population and find their own food. They were not welcome in our house, but stayed in their place: outside.

As Wally was learning to talk, Mom had acquired two special long-haired kittens. Dad had finally relented, and the kittens became our first indoor pets. One was white and the other gray, and when they arrived, they had no names. We began to refer to them as the "white one" and the "gray one." Not very practiced at naming cats, we soon named one "Whitey." (Maybe we thought about the radio newsman we often heard on WNAX Yankton, South Dakota, named Whitey Larson. Or maybe it was just the cat's color.) The other one became "Grapefruit," because that was what Wally heard when we spoke of "the gray one." The cat's name became a family reminder of a toddler's learning to talk.

Wally didn't get as much opportunity to take care of farm animals as the rest of us. But in the spring he was four, we got the five *bum lambs*, given away because the mothers couldn't or wouldn't care for them. Wally learned to helped nurse the lambs with bottles of milk until they were able to eat grass and weeds. The next year, however, Wally became the target of one of two males who had matured into a mean ram. The castrating process, using a heavy rubber band Dad had placed on him, had failed. No one else was attacked, but Wally was frightened and tried to avoid the animal as it freely roamed our place.

On one of our trips to Oregon, which usually took about two weeks every other year, we visited a small sea aquarium in Depoe Bay. In a memorable moment Wally interacted with a small seal. He was stooping to a window in the pool wall near the ground and making eye contact with a little seal on the other side of the glass. The rest of us were looking at larger seals from above, while the observant little boy and the curious little seal were studying each other below.

When we moved to Oregon, Wally started kindergarten as I began high school. The opportunities to observe and enjoy our little brother were reduced. That first year, each of us four children was in a different school with our own activities and new friends to get to know. Wally completed third grade the year I graduated from high school and then went off to college. So, I missed much involvement with him in his preteen and teenage years. I heard he was a whiz in high school. He could read a book while the teacher was lecturing but never miss giving the right answer—even when she called on him to catch him not paying attention.

Wally started high school a year after my 1967 marriage in Georgia, and I was attending Princeton Theological Seminary in New Jersey. He graduated from college in 1973, a few months before my oldest son was born in Cincinnati, Ohio. We lived on opposite sides of the country. So, when I was a young adult, my sister Crystal gave me a challenge,

"You need to spend more time with Wally—you don't even know him!" Although we have never lived near one another since I was in high school, I have made a point of visiting with him whenever possible and getting to know him better.

Most of the growing-up experiences that shaped our worldviews were different. My early homelife and schooling were definitely rural while Wally's were more urban. Nevertheless, I am always impressed when I recognize how similar some of our adult paths have been. My work took me to serve a Native American community in Alaska, and about the same time in Wally's career with Bonneville Power, he became the go-to person for negotiation with the Eastern Oregon Native tribes.

Both of us put in countless hours growing home gardens, practicing composting and organic gardening. These shared interests surprised me when I discovered them, but undoubtedly they were inherited from our dad, who became an avid town gardener after he left the farm. I am proud of who Wally became—a husband, a father, and an attorney who studied economics. He has made his career in the major public power company in Portland, Oregon.

Wally about 2 years old.

Wally as an infant with
the swoop hairdo
his siblings loved to produce.

Dad and Wally visiting the site of a local train wreck—
not a common occurrence in our area.

PART E

How We Lived

PART 3

How We Lived

TWENTY-SIX

One Hundred Sixteen Bullheads and One Colander

My brother Gene and I were best playmates—always scheming new diversions on our prairie farm. We could always fish for bass, bluegills, and bullheads in small dams nearby, and occasionally we did. I can't remember Dad ever fishing; it was Mom who taught us to put a worm on a hook, cast it into the water with a bamboo pole and watch the red and white bobber for a nibble or a bite. It could sometimes a be a long wait.

I was eleven and Gene nine the summer of 1954 when we had an unusual fishing adventure. A few hundred yards down the hill from our house was the pond—a stunning view from our house. Soil excavated from the dry creek had become the earthen dam that was filled by spring snowmelt and occasional heavy summer rains. Excess water flowed over a dirt spillway a little higher than the original path of the nameless creek. A few hundred feet downstream from this outlet, the water fell about six feet into the terrain of the natural creek bed. As it flowed over this drop-off, it began eroding the soil and forming a gully.

Dad invented and installed a solution he called the "trickle tube," an elbow of two-foot diameter corrugated steel culvert material. Instead of

189

rushing over the dirt bank, the water swirled into the tube's vertical five-foot top section and gushed out its three-foot horizontal bottom. It was fascinating to watch, and it worked—no more gully. But an unexpected side affect appeared: a small pool was created by the circling water coming out the bottom. It became a pool two or three feet deep and about twenty feet in diameter. Large in the spring, this pool evaporated over the summer leaving dry dirt. Gene and I enjoyed trying to catch frogs as long as the water was there. They would watch us coming, then jump in when we approached; we never caught a frog.

On a late summer day, as this puddle was shrinking, we noticed there were many small fish in it. They had come over the spillway and were trapped in the shrinking puddle. If we couldn't catch frogs, maybe we could catch the fish. Instead of poles and hooks we borrowed Mom's kitchen colander. Mom may not have understood what we were going to do with it, but she let us use it. She had two younger children to take care of, so we were on our own that afternoon.

Barefoot, wearing cutoff jeans and no tops, we entered the water with the colander as our net. The pool was so small and there were so many fish they couldn't avoid us. The more we tromped in the water the muddier it got. It became impossible to see the fish and hard for them to see us. Surely the oxygen became scarce in the muddy water, and any fish we missed probably died a little sooner than they would have, waiting for the puddle to dry up.

The fish who had come down the trickle tube were young, most not over six inches long. They were bullheads, a small variety of scaleless, bony catfish with sharp protective protrusions on either side of their mouths—the *cat whiskers* that give the species its name. Picking them up with bare hands was an invitation to be punctured, and it happened many times that day. When we were finished, we counted one hundred-sixteen. We had been successful and had something to brag about to cousins and young uncles at church the next Sunday.

When it was time to take our bounty home, the water was so murky we had no idea where the colander was. We searched frantically, then reluctantly had to admit we'd lost it. Mom scolded us soundly, but nothing could be done. It was gone.

While exuberantly fishing, neither of us remembered Mom's rule that whoever catches the fish cleans them. We had expended much energy capturing them, then searching for the colander, and finally carrying home the buckets with our harvest. Now we had to cut off the heads, gut every fish, and wrap them in waxed paper—not nearly as much fun as catching them and even more tiring.

Our kitchen had its kerosene refrigerator by that time, so none of the fish were wasted. We enjoyed many bullhead breakfasts, dinners, and suppers completely unaware that some people consider bullheads too bony for serious anglers. We considered ourselves serious enough!

The next spring, to our surprise, the colander showed up again to retake its place in Mom's kitchen. She had done without it during much of a year, and no replacement had been purchased. Its adventure had changed its appearance. The colander had settled into mud that dried around it, causing a chemical reaction in the aluminum. About half of it had blackened.

Seasons came and went, and the taste of the fish left our mouths, but in Mom's kitchen the discolored colander was used until she gave up housekeeping forty years later. Perhaps she had looked at it with amusement. Her little boys had grown up and gone off on their own, but the blackened utensil recalled their childhood adventure and all those bullheads she had to incorporate into days of family meals.

Almost seventy years later, our sister Crystal, too young to have joined our adventure in 1954, uses the still-discolored colander in her own kitchen. Perhaps it reminds her of her brothers' unusual experience, or of how many little fish we all ate. But maybe she sees Mom's colander just the way she has always remembered it.

Jim and Gene cleaning the 116 bullheads in the back yard.

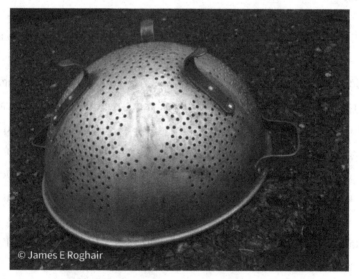

© James E Roghair

The lost and found colander that caught the
bullheads—at least six decades later.

TWENTY-SEVEN

Is a Picture Worth a Thousand Words?

A *picture is worth a thousand words*. The cliché seems to suggest that no picture needs an explanation. But there are two pictures in our family that mask a secret.

In my home is a gild-framed, colored photograph about seventeen inches high, twelve inches across in the middle, but only nine inches at the top and bottom. It has a sort of oval shape, pleasant to the eye and slightly elegant, but not lavish. An heirloom portrait.

In the picture are two innocent-looking, blond, fair-skinned boys, about two and four years old. They are wearing shorts with fabric suspenders and short-sleeved dress shirts. The younger one is seated on a stool, and on his feet are white socks and brown sandals. The older child stands with an arm around the shoulders and a hand on the knee of the younger. It is a friendly pose. Their sweet smiles make this a cherubic portrait.

Were we cherubs, my brother Gene and I? That is surely not the way I remember us in our growing years. Best friends? Yes, most of the time. But angels? Not often. The photograph was taken professionally in a studio in Pierre, South Dakota, sometime before our sister Crystal was born in the summer of 1947.

Today in Crystal's home is a similar color portrait in a matching frame, a little girl about four years old standing alone. Her brown hair fluffs a little, and she wears a blouse with a blue pattern print. This picture was taken in a rather unusual setting—in the Murdo locker plant, where rural folks took butchered meat to be packaged, frozen, and stored in their individual rented lockers. Perhaps the photographer was starting a new business but didn't have his own studio, yet. The pose he captured may not be as intentionally cherubic as is the boys' picture. But the little girl is engaging, and the viewer is drawn to her. This is a portrait of Crystal.

These portraits tell their story, but what they do not tell may be more interesting. They were made in the early 1950s while we were still living on our Okaton farm. I was about eight. Dad was working hard to eke out a living on his small acreage.

Much of the time, Mom was at home with her three kids. The gardening, cooking and homemaking did not hide the silence of the open prairie. It was different from the small town of Timber Lake where she had grown up, less than one hundred and fifty miles north of Okaton. Her town was no metropolis, but her family's store and home had filled their lives with a constant flow of buyers, sellers, and boarders. There were Sioux Indians and Whites—farmers, ranchers, trappers, and travelers. It was the kind of life an outgoing child had thrived on. By contrast, surely Mother found her life as a farm wife lonely at times. There was no commercial phone service, no electricity, and certainly no television or other electronic connection. Just the one, huge, battery-powered radio which could receive a few stations. Mom was largely cut off from the rest of the world for most of each week.

Since there were so few visitors to the farm, it was exciting when a travelling salesman showed up. Those men were in a position to provide a human link that farm women like our mother missed. During their unannounced visits they could often sell something, and it was easy to spot their wares in our neighbors' homes as well as ours.

One day a salesman came to sell portraits. Give him black and white photographs, and he would have them enlarged. He would have them colored in beautiful natural hues. He would bring them back in golden frames. That was what he would do, and as a bonus he would throw in a similarly framed color photo of South Dakota's famous four presidents on Mount Rushmore.

He sold Mother on his services, and she gave him four small photos to be turned into heirloom portraits. I do not know the price of the four portraits, probably less than one hundred dollars, but this was the 1950s, and a hundred dollars was a lot of money. Mom wrote a check on the joint account at the Okaton State Bank. The salesman left, pleased with his work and eager to find another lonely housewife.

Dad was normally quite easy-going, but that afternoon when he arrived home after many hours in the field, he discovered what an extravagant purchase Mom had made. He became uncharacteristically angry. He got on the party line using the battery-powered crank phone and called the store in Okaton. He was patched into the commercial phone line to reach the bank. He stopped the check. No portraits!

Mom must have felt awful.

In a short time, the salesman, unable to cash his check, showed up at our farm, again unannounced. His personality and salesmanship were undaunted. I do not remember what he said to Dad; perhaps I did not even hear it. Dad probably took him out to the car to discuss the matter privately. But before the salesman had finished his work, he had convinced Dad that the family needed at least two of the four portraits.

He would still include the bonus Mount Rushmore print. All in a day's work for the salesman!

Perhaps Mom felt at least partially vindicated.

Over the years, I have thought of this salesman's persistence and his success. How often did that scenario play out? An angry husband has to be sold on the same things the wife has already bought. Were his tactics with the men the same as with the women? I wonder.

About three-quarters of a century after their purchase my sister and I display the framed portraits. I am not sure what became of the bonus picture of Mount Rushmore. When we were doing a final cleanup of Mom and Dad's apartment in 1996, Gene didn't want the angelic portrait of him and me, so I took it and display it in my office. I enjoy seeing it. Perhaps Gene did not remember drama of its origin as clearly as I.

Crystal's picture hangs in a conspicuous place in her home, but she doesn't remember the circumstances of obtaining the colored portraits. Her memory is that when the original black and white photo was taken, her shirt was actually a bright red on white print, not blue. Did the salesman get the coloring instructions wrong, or did the person doing the tinting have a better idea?

As Dad and Mom got older, they always had these two portraits in a conspicuous place in their home. I doubt that they ever spoke of the circumstances surrounding their acquisition; better to let sleeping dogs lie. I wonder how they individually remembered the incident.

Our youngest brother Wallace was born after the time of the portrait salesman. So he never had the opportunity to be featured in a similar heirloom. All he knows of these pictures is what we siblings have told him.

Now, I've shared more than a thousand words to tell the story that the pictures themselves cannot tell.

Jim & Gene in the gilded frame heirloom portrait.

Crystal in her matching portrait.

TWENTY-EIGHT

The Blizzard of 1952:
Before, During, After

Before the Storm

The blizzard of 1952 is legendary in western South Dakota. Everyone who lived through it has a story to tell. I was nearly nine years old, a third grader, and my brother Gene almost seven in first grade. I clearly remember the experience of this horrendous storm as well as what I heard others say about it.

It was Monday morning, January 21, 1952; Dad drove Gene and me to the Okaton School. For midwinter, it was a warm and beautiful day. A few huge snowflakes floated gently to the ground. There was no wind or any hint of bad weather. So we took the 1949 Ford car instead of the four-wheel drive Willys Jeep we usually used in the winter.

Since the day was so mild, we didn't even dress in our usual three layers of winter clothes. We wore the woolen long-johns and blue jeans, but not our denim bib overalls—dark blue for Gene and striped blue and white for me. We normally wore the outer layer on the way to school and stripped it off when we got there—but not on that beautiful morning.

We did wear our overshoes, warm coats, mittens, and caps with earflaps. How pleasant the weather was that morning is imprinted on my memory.

After leaving Gene and me at the school door, Dad went a few blocks to the general store/post office to get the mail and, as was his custom, to chat with relatives and neighbors before heading home. His brother Nicholas Albert (our uncle Albert) was there. He had heard a weather report on KOTA radio, Rapid City, a little over one hundred miles west. "The snow is heavy there," he said, "with a strong west wind. It's gonna be a big one, and it's headed our way." Uncle Albert, who had no kids in school yet, advised his older brother, "Go get your kids, and take 'em home." Dad took the warning and was back at the school within minutes. He advised the two teachers of the coming storm, but since they had the responsibility for fifteen or twenty kids and no way to contact parents, they went on with their lessons for the time being.

When we started home the falling snowflakes were still large and beautiful but becoming denser. It was only three and a half miles home, but there were no farmhouses along the way. Our first mile was mostly on the original US Highway 16 built in the 1940s, but the second mile was under reconstruction. Old pavement was torn up and we had to share the unfinished dirt and gravel with earth moving machines and especially with gravel trucks.

At thirty-nine, Dad was always a careful driver, but this was a dangerous situation. We entered the construction zone, with no wind, but the snowfall had become so heavy it was getting hard to see where we were going. I was in the middle of the front seat, and Gene was sitting by the passenger door. Dad said, "Guys, this is going to be hard. Gene, I want you to watch on your side of the road. Look for the wooden construction stakes to make sure we don't run off that side of the road. Jim, I want you to look straight ahead. Tell me if you see a gravel truck coming. I will watch the left side of the road." Gene and I watched carefully, and Gene reported the position of the stakes as we went by. I only saw one gravel truck and warned Dad as it approached. Whether Dad was relying on us for our safety or just trying to keep us occupied to avoid panic, I don't know. But together we crept along that road without incident.

After the mile of construction, we relaxed a little as we turned north onto the more familiar and less hazardous mile of Jones County dirt road. After safely navigating it, we turned west onto a narrower township dirt road, which we would take only a half mile before our own two-hundred-yard driveway, the final segment of this journey.

When we were within an eighth of a mile of the driveway, Dad, disoriented by the falling snow, mistook a snowbank on the right side of the road for one on the left. He drove directly into a deep drift from an earlier snowfall. He knew immediately the car was stuck, so wasted no time trying to get it free. There was nothing to do but pile out of the car and begin trudging home.

The low visibility made even walking treacherous. But finally, we were triumphantly walking between the well-known two rows of scrubby Russian olive trees lining our driveway and onto our home place. As soon as we were within sight of the house, Dad said sternly, "Get into the house right now. I am going to make sure the horse and the cows are safe in the barn and shut the door." We did as we were told.

When we burst through the door, Mom, with four-and-a-half-year-old Crysti by her side, asked, "Why are you guys home?" She had not heard a weather report and had not been outdoors. "Mom," I said, "a blizzard is coming! Dad picked us up at school." Gene chimed in, "There is so much snow. The car is stuck in a snowbank, and we had to walk home!" Before we could tell her everything, Dad came in from the barn.

On his way back to the house, Dad had observed the Wincharger on its wooden tower turning lazily. Then it abruptly indicated the storm had arrived: "The Wincharger just swung around," he said. "It's a strong wind from the west. This is going to be a big blizzard!" With a sigh of relief Dad took off his overshoes and coat. He did not mention that had we been a few minutes later getting home, we might not have made it. Or that if he had run off the road a little further from our driveway, we might still be walking.

Driving and walking in the heavy snow had been difficult, but that was minor compared to the hazard of blowing snow in a strong wind—actual blizzard conditions. In such a storm anyone can be disoriented, even in a space as familiar as between our house and the barn. Dad rarely expressed strong emotions, but I'm sure he offered up a silent prayer of thanks for the safety of home and the close call we had avoided.

Perhaps Mom, about six and a half months pregnant, imagined what it would have been like to be stranded with her little girl and not know where the rest of her family was. She gave us all hugs and asked, "Who would like a cup of hot chocolate?"

During the Storm

Mom was thirty-five that winter. She had taught school for only one year before she and Dad were married, and they moved to the farm. But like an experienced elementary teacher, she was always prepared to entertain children when we were cooped up in the house for long hours, or even days. I particularly remember cutting out pictures from catalogues and magazines, especially those related to farming. We could arrange and rearrange the pictures as we wished all over the living room to create imaginary stories or scenes.

Mom got out paper dolls just when they were needed so we could dress them and populate our scenes. Perhaps we needed a little refereeing to stay out of each other's way, but the living room seemed big enough for us to each have our space. If we got tired of setting up the temporary scenes, we might cut out pictures and paste them more permanently into scrapbooks. There were also board games such as Uncle Wiggly and card games like hearts or Rook. We kids kept busy and for the most part got along.

If all else failed, Mom would discover that she needed a cup of ingredients to be prepared for cooking. In the attic there was always a bag of hard-shelled black walnuts with the thick husks already removed—brought back from a trip to the West Coast. When kids needed a project, she would get out the bag and find what we used as an anvil—the ten-inch piece of steel railroad track Dad had salvaged from somewhere. She gave us a hammer, a nut pick, and a cup and put us to work. We learned to hit the nuts on the stem end to get the best access to the meat inside, but we always had to dig with the pick to retrieve the tiny edible bits. We tried to avoid getting pieces of shell into the cup, but some always made it into the baking anyway.

While Gene and I were busy with the shelling, Crysti helped get ready for the baking. Mom was good about including all of us in the kitchen, and we all learned to cook. We always enjoyed the cookies or cake that included the walnuts—even before they were baked. We licked the stirring spoon and scraped the dough from the inside of the mixing bowl. The work of getting the nuts ready seemed like time well spent. At that age, however, I didn't realize how effective the project was to distract us from the boredom of being stuck in the house.

Dad was the best at whiling away hours waiting out a storm. Having only finished the eighth grade, he was nevertheless an avid reader. He would read almost anything and was then prepared to carry on a conversation on any subject. Regardless of the noise of three kids running around the house, he sat in his chair, often with the radio playing, yet so absorbed in his reading that he might not even respond if we spoke to him. Mom spent hours in the kitchen, since being in a storm did not interfere with our appetites or expectations for regular meals. She also did a little sewing or mending but didn't have much time for other distractions.

During this blizzard, our telephone rang several times. It was the battery-powered crank telephone that Dad had installed and hooked up to a line with ten or fifteen of our neighbors. Since the whole system was one party line and totally powered by the dry cell batteries in each phone, every phone rang for any call. Although everyone knew who was getting a call and might be curious to hear the conversation, we normally did not listen to the calls for others. It would be impolite to be a *rubberneck*. But during the storm those rules did not apply.

The van Rooyen home was on US 16, and in the blizzard a number of travelers became stranded there. Luckily one vehicle was a bread truck, so at least there was food to share with the houseful of people. Although the Grandview one-room school was a few hundred feet away from that house, I never heard that any of them took refuge in it. But the stuck travelers wanted to be in touch with family in distant places to let them know they were safe. So van Rooyens called the Okaton store four or five miles away. The store/post office had the only phone in Okaton on our party line, and provided a connection to the larger Bell Telephone system. Mae Conger, who lived with her sister Ann Williams in an apartment in the back, owned and operated the store. She was also post mistress, and occasionally telephone operator.

During the storm, whenever we heard a call for the store, Dad picked it up. Van Rooyens and their guests were having trouble conversing with Mae in the store, but Dad, about halfway between, could hear better and he relayed the messages. We recognized during that storm what an advantage it was to have even such a primitive phone system.

The blizzard that started Monday morning continued until Tuesday evening, but eventually even such a big storm comes to an end. We had been cooped up in the house for two days. Our driveway and the roads connected to it were still impassable because of snowdrifts six or more feet high.

When the sun came out Wednesday, it was a glorious day. It was still cold, but to Mom's relief, we kids bundled up and went outside. We discovered where the big snow drifts were and scrambled over them. We found our old sled, our toboggan, and the large steel butcher's tray Mom let us use, and we went sliding down the hill near our front door to the edge of the frozen dam. We expended much pent-up energy walking up the hill to slide down again. It was exhilarating. We didn't think about the cold but absorbed the sunshine and had a great time.

About the same time as we went sledding, Dad decided he should mount our old horse, Boots, and ride bareback into Okaton. I'm not sure there was any particular piece of mail he had to get, or any item of groceries needed. Rather, riding the horse into town after the blizzard was a way of expressing that the storm had not stopped him; he and his family were well and accounted for. We had more days to wait before a big Caterpillar D-8 with a snowplow blade came to push the snow to the side and open our roads. We watched with excitement when the huge machine finally came roaring down our driveway to liberate us.

After the Storm

As we became reconnected to our community we learned about the experiences of family, friends, and neighbors. Dad's brother Jacob (our uncle Jack) was building a new house for his wife Grace and their family four or five miles from Okaton, and at about that distance from where they were currently living. His oldest son, my cousin Melvin, who had graduated from eighth grade, was no longer in school and was working with him. When they realized a blizzard was coming, they started home but didn't get there. They stayed at Grandpa and Grandma's nearer Okaton, but still about a mile from their own home.

Wally Scouten, the depot agent (who took care of all ticketing, freight, and other railroad business except track repair) lived with his family in an apartment in the depot. As the storm was developing, he went to the school to rescue the teachers and children. The kids who lived in town had already gone home before the storm became severe, but the teachers were still there with my cousins because no one had come to pick them up. The depot agent escorted Jack and Grace's three girls, Alice, Lois and Lorraine, and the teacher Mrs. Schroll, to the temporary trailer camp that was close to the school. Mr. Scouten then came back and took Jack and Grace's sons Richard and Lawrence and the other teacher, Mrs. Gilbert, to her home. Since there were no phones, my aunt, uncle, and cousins had no way to communicate with the each other in their four different locations.

Aunt Grace, home alone, had no idea where the rest of her family was. After the wind stopped, but before the roads were plowed, Jack and Melvin went home to check on Grace. They walked about a mile over the snowbanks and were relieved to find she was safe. She had gone out to the barn to milk the cow during her lonely wait. She was happy to see her husband and oldest son, and her happiness was complete when she was finally reunited with the other five children who had waited out the storm about two miles away in town.

The morning the blizzard started, on the road near where they were working, Jack and Melvin had seen four neighbors, Pete Judd, forty-eight, his nephew Cecil Judd, twenty-one, and Pete's daughters Flora, eight, and Helen, nine, whom they had picked up from the one-room rural Scovil School. Their teacher had pleaded with them to shelter at the school, but likely Pete felt he had no choice; he was concerned about his wife Helen at home with their infant daughter, Alma Kay, and he was determined to be with them. It was a fateful choice. When Jack and Melvin saw them, they had stopped to assist another neighbor who had run off the road. Since the Judds had several miles to drive, Jack encouraged them to keep going.

Pete and Cecil had probably picked up the girls at about the same time Dad took Gene and me from the Okaton School, before the wind had come up. Similar to our experience of abandoning our car and walking home, the engine of their Jeep had drowned out with the moisture of the heavy snow. The Judds left it and started walking home.

The Mother, Helen Judd and her baby had waited out the storm at home, as had Aunt Grace, and as our own mother and sister Crysti might have. When the storm was over, Helen courageously strapped her infant onto a small sled and pulled her to a neighbor's home to seek help.

Although we had arrived safely at home before the wind came up, none of our four neighbors made it. When the snowplow finally came to clear the roads, four bodies were discovered. The girls Flora and Helen were found closest to the Jeep. Their father had apparently been with them when they succumbed but could do nothing to help; their mittens were unexplainably in his coat pocket. He went on but was overcome closer to home. Cecil was even nearer to safety, within yards of the house; the often-repeated truth was confirmed that in such storms people may not find their way, even in familiar places.

I did not know Flora and Helen well, and our families were not close. But I had competed with them at school rally days along with other kids from the tiny schools in our third of the county. It was hard to believe the girls were not going to be there for our next annual event. Their deaths were the first of anyone my age that I had experienced. I had known of adults who died: the young father of a family in the church died of a heart attack, and Dad had taken me to the funeral of the elderly husband of my piano teacher. But I was not prepared for the death of children I knew.

Our parents tried to reassure us. We did not know the Judd family well enough to go to the funeral or visit their home, but nevertheless the impact on my family was great. When I recently shared a draft of this story with my sister Crysti, she was not happy to be reminded of the painful memories she still had regarding the deaths. At the age of four and a half she had found the deaths difficult to cope with and had been unable to share her feelings with anyone else.

The frightful blizzard of 1952 was indeed one to remember. Reliving it in my memory over the years, I know it was the beginning of a growing recognition of the fragility of human life—of how close our own escape had been, and how near death could be. I gained a lasting respect for the capriciousness of weather.

Now in my senior years, I still remember Helen and Flora as little girls. I ponder how full my life has been, but how short theirs were. I recognize more now than I did at the time how easily the blizzard experiences of our family and the Judd's might have been reversed. Whether I attribute the turn of events to divine providence or to blind fate, my response is gratitude and recognition of how important it is to make the most of the gift of our days.

Flora Judd on her 8th birthday in January 1952. She died with her sister, father and a cousin in the January blizzard. (Photo from Ancestry.com with permission)

Helen Judd on her 9th birthday in January 1952. She died in the blizzard with others in her family. (Photo from Ancestry. com with permission.)

Mother wrote on back of this picture, "January or February 1952. One of several times our driveway was cleared. Johnnie Daum in snowplow."

Mom wrote on back, "Jimmy's 9th birthday holding new co-op tractor." This was the first non-John Deere toy I had received—a Cockshutt, sold by Farmer's Union Cooperatives and painted orange. Was Dad preparing me for tractor brand changes?

TWENTY-NINE

Potholder Memories

In the late twentieth and early twenty-first centuries, many have come to feel rather proud of the personal and community practices of recycling. It's almost as if we had discovered something genuinely new that we could pat ourselves on the back for. But I am reminded of the example set by my mother and by my grandmothers—Cornelia Roghair born in 1889 and Crystal Bowder born in 1891. We learned to recycle from them. In the 1950s both grandmas were in their sixties—quite old I thought then, although now that I am about eighty I perceive age differently. But that perception is not all that has changed; the now progressive, and seemingly innovative, activity of recycling was a natural part of life for my grandparents. It was what they did and how we were taught—not something people needed to be cajoled into.

I saw Grandma Roghair several times a week since we lived only about four miles apart. She was the mother of twelve children who lived to adulthood. In my earliest memory, more than half of those children were still living at home with her and Grandpa. She was a western South Dakota Dutch farm wife. Her ancestry surely contributed to her meticulous housekeeping and frugal ways. Beds were made, floors were swept, and everything was put in order early every day. Grandma and her daughters always prepared meals as the men and boys, including Grandpa and their two youngest sons, still living at home when I was a child, did the farm work.

The three main meals of the day were called *breakfast, dinner,* and *supper,* but there were also two regular and ritualized snack times, a mid-morning *coffee time* and a mid-afternoon *lunch.* This meant gathering five times a day around the kitchen table. If one or more of the men were working at a distance from the house, it might be necessary to get morning coffee and afternoon snack out to them, and possibly even the noontime dinner if they couldn't take time to come in from the field.

Homemaking and housework were the highest priority for Grandma Roghair and her daughters. Whatever housework could be done in the early morning was soon accomplished, and then there was time for Grandma to work on the things that surely brought her joy. She crocheted and knitted. She made rugs, quilts, and afghans, recycling worn-out and discarded clothing. Although her output was high, I don't think she ever sold anything. She gave her creations away to family and friends. Grandma was reusing things that might have been thrown out, and many people benefited from her work.

Today in our kitchen in Santa Fe, New Mexico, we have a set of four small, tightly crocheted potholders, six inches in diameter, round, and white with a colored string decoration—a daily reminder of Grandma Roghair. These particular potholders were given to me by my mother after my first marriage—my mother was good about keeping things and labelling them to pass on from generation to generation. When these pieces came into my possession, they were special to me. I put them away, and we didn't use them for many years. But more recently, after my first wife's death in 1994, and I was remarried, I thought, *What am I saving these for?* With no good answer, the potholders went into daily use.

I can't be absolutely certain when Grandma Roghair made these four potholders, but my guess is they were made in the mid-1950s, based on my presumed recognition of the raw materials from which they were made.

On those materials hang the rest of this story, and Grandma Bowder enters my tale. Her life and routine were not as rigidly ordered as Grandma Roghair's. She too was the mother of a large family—all nine of her children lived to adulthood. In my earliest memories, only her youngest daughter, Norma Jane, was still living with her and Grandpa in their Salem, Oregon, home. Their life together had not been completely smooth. They had closed their grocery and general store in the small town of Timber Lake, South Dakota, and moved to Salem, Oregon, during World War II. About ten years later Grandma, by then in her mid-sixties, was working as a maid in the YMCA in Salem. I now understand that making beds and cleaning rooms was a daily drudgery for her, but to us, her grandkids living on our isolated farm in South Dakota, Grandma's work seemed exciting—maybe even exotic.

In her role as the maid of the Y, she was also its lost and found department. She had the responsibility, after a certain length of time, to dispose of anything left in the rooms. Thus, Grandma came into possession of a lot of stuff that residents—on the move as they often were—simply abandoned and never returned to claim. These items became hers to do with as she pleased.

Without fail, every Christmas during that era, Grandma Bowder packed up and sent us a large cardboard box filled with things she had acquired. (Actually, it was usually nearer New Year's Day that it arrived in our little Post Office.) The box was brought home and eagerly opened on the kitchen floor. In it we found shirts, socks, jeans, and caps. There were also pocketknives, watches, and trinkets of all sorts. Some things Grandma had labeled for one or another of the four kids or for our parents. Other items were to be divided up as our family saw fit. The contents of Grandma's boxes were always exciting—maybe even more than the new gifts we actually got on Christmas day. We enjoyed putting the various items to use immediately. But there was also the packing material, tangled gobs of cotton string a foot or two in length.

All the clean sheets Grandma put on the beds in the Y were laundered commercially and returned in bundles tied with string. No plastic bags, shrink wrap, or mailing tape—it was string every day. The accumulating pieces of strimg were deposited helter-skelter into a container, scooped up, taken home, and stored by Grandma. She used the string to fill all unoccupied space in her boxes. I do not know what percentage of the Y's yearly string accumulation came to our house, but it must have been significant.

As soon as the gifts from Grandma Bowder were divided up, Mom made sure we remembered our next job. It was to untangle the packing string and roll it into balls. We didn't tie the lengths together, just added them individually to a ball until it reached three or four inches in diameter. It took us weeks, maybe months, to get all of the string untangled and balled. Then as soon as we had some balls ready, we took them to Grandma Roghair, and she went to work. The cotton string was transformed from waste into various items—most memorably, the potholders she crocheted.

She also crocheted soaker pants for babies. In the time before disposable diapers and plastic pants, Grandma's soaker pants were an absorbent garment that fit over baby diapers. No new mother we knew would leave home without them. They were made from wool: I wonder where she got the yarn to make these pants—maybe from unravelling old sweaters or worn-out socks.

To remember my grandmothers, decades after the deaths, I do not have any soaker pants, only the four potholders. Three of mine have blue string worked into the edges as decoration and one red. Washed over and over these potholders seem to be indestructible. The fibers will likely outlast my lifetime, so I wonder if anyone else will ever want to use them.

My mother and grandmothers were not recycling pioneers. There was nothing heroic or particularly unusual about the way my mother facilitated the cycle, or how one grandma collected and the other made use of waste materials. They were all simply using their own skills, opportunities, and imaginations to live responsibly in their own time and place. They were just "making do," using what they had for the benefit of their families and neighbors—and letting nothing go to waste.

We who try to carefully recycle things in our time might be encouraged by the thriftiness and ingenuity of our forebears. I am proud to be descended from such self-sufficient and creative people and hope to pass on that legacy. The potholders are nothing less than daily reminders of where we as a family come from and the life examples that were set for us.

My four grandparents: from left Henry and Cornelia Roghair, Crystal and Frank Bowder, all in their mid-sixties. This spring 1952 photo was taken in the Roghair home near Okaton, South Dakota. The Bowders were visiting from Oregon to assist our family at the time of the birth of their mutual grandchild, my brother Wallace. Although these two couples were not close friends, during later years (mid-1960s to early 1970s), whenever I visited Grandma Roghair in her Okaton home, a small, framed copy of this picture had been placed on her kitchen table. I later realized that she kept it handy so she could put it out when I was coming. It wasn't there permanently. Their long-distance collaboration on potholders had not created a strong personal bond between my grandmas.

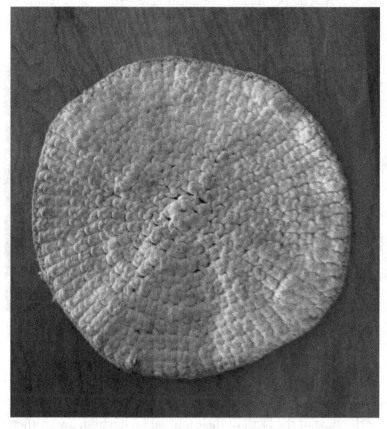

One of the potholders made by Grandma Roghair,
likely from materials Grandma Bowder supplied.

THIRTY

A Twelve-Year-Old One-way Operator

In 1951, Dad purchased a Minneapolis-Moline Universal tractor (the U). It was painted prairie gold, an orange-yellow color, and a clear deviation from his family's always-green, John Deere preference. Dad had initiated that tradition himself in the late 1930s, and it had hitherto been strictly adhered to by the rest of his family. He bought the U from Jeff Sanderson, owner of a dry-goods general store in Murdo. Jeff had had limited success attempting to add farm machinery to his business, and the tractor sat on his lot for a long time. During one of his always-extended conversations with Jeff, Dad negotiated the purchase of the U. He undoubtedly got a good deal for taking the inventory off his friend's lot.

Dad's family had become so loyal to John Deere that he was now getting ribbed by his brothers and nephews for committing the unthinkable—buying *that* tractor. Even Gene and I, about nine and eleven, found it hard to imagine why Dad had brought home such a stranger. We took the attitude of our cousins and uncles.

Shortly after he brought the new tractor home, he was doing the springtime plowing of the vegetable garden between our house and the dam. It was early in the season, and the ground was still a little wet from the snowmelt. He got the tractor stuck in the mud. But instead of trying

217

to be helpful or even sympathetic, we little copy-cats stood there mocking our dad the way we thought our cousins might. We shouted at him that his tractor was no good. In his frustration—not only for getting stuck, but for our impertinence—he yelled angrily at us to leave him alone. It was such a rarity for Dad to show anger that we actually did leave him alone.

Gradually we got used to the tractor. The next year, when I was twelve, I was ready to assist with the summer field work and drive the U. Dad would not need a hired man that summer, and I could take any ribbing from the cousins that might still be coming. My work week was five or six days, and my daily hours about five or six. I got time off to go to 4-H events and other important things, but I was proud of the responsibility of handling a big tractor and doing a major part of the yearly work in the fields of summer fallow—the land that was not planted that year but would be in wheat the following year.

The implement I was pulling was a Krause one-way disc plow, which we simply called the *one-way*. It was a modified version of a plow and related to a disc harrow. Fifteen or so sharp concave steel discs, each nearly three feet in diameter and closely spaced on a single shaft, were mounted at an angle on a three-wheeled carriage with rubber tires. The discs rotated as they were pulled through the dirt and moved the topsoil from the left to the right. The tractor's hydraulic system was connected to a lift that could raise the discs for transporting or maneuvering through irregular spaces. This machine had much larger discs than the normal disc harrows, or simply *discs* as we called them, which had smaller blades and moved dirt in both directions. I was already familiar with the one-way; we had had it as long as I could remember. It didn't seem complicated or dangerous to me.

I knew I had to start going around the outside of the field and work my way into the middle. The main thing to remember was to keep the right front tire of the tractor in the furrow created by the one-way on its previous round, so no unnecessary furrow was left. The U was much easier to use with the one-way than Dad's John Deere model A would have been. The U's front wheels were spaced apart like the rear wheels. Most of the John Deeres in our area were really row crop or *tricycle* models, so-called because their two front tires were placed close together in the center. Having the front wheels apart made it easy to gauge how to keep the one-way rounds properly spaced, covering the furrow of the previous round. I probably couldn't have managed to keep the one-way aligned with a tricycle John Deere. I wonder if Dad had my one-way driving in mind when he purchased the Minneapolis-Moline; I certainly did not think of that possibility at the time.

Dad's instructions the morning he took me out for my first day of one-waying weren't much more comprehensive than those he gave me the first time I drove the Jeep home four years earlier. All I remember is, "Now, I want you to always keep your legs over this bar—one leg on either side." The padded seat was attached to a single steel bar so it could swing to the right or the left, and the operator could even drive while standing up on one side of the seat or the other. But my instructions were clear: my feet were to remain on either side of the bar—on the seat and no standing. I obeyed, as I was accustomed to do. I didn't question why, or even consider Dad's reasoning. I proudly spent the summer one-waying.

It wasn't until years later, when I had a child of my own, that I thought about my early experience. Finally, in a flash of insight, I realized why Dad had given me such clear instructions. Trailing closely behind the tractor, the one-way's large sharp discs were cutting the soil. Had I fallen off the moving tractor, it would have been mere seconds before I was cut into a number of pieces by the rotating steel. Keeping my legs on either side of the steel bar that held the seat was my insurance—to keep me from falling off. I did keep my legs in place, and I had a safe summer.

In twenty-first century America, I wonder if a farm kid would be given the role of pulling a one-way with no more protection than the position of his legs. Today, small children are carefully strapped into car seats, and everyone uses seat belts in their cars. Gone are the days when such simple instructions could be considered sufficient. But I am proud that I was deemed responsible for my own safety at such a young age.

Perhaps Dad's childhood experiences led him to trust his own children. Dad never became much of a writer—only a few handwritten memories of his youth and family life remain and a few typed notes dictated to Mom. One of his noted experiences seems significant. Before they moved to South Dakota, Dad's family lived on a northwest Iowa farm. His family and most of their neighbors spoke one dialect or another of Dutch or a mixture, although they had to speak English in school starting in World War I.

At the age of seven, probably in the spring or summer of 1920, Dad was sent out to the field with the hired man, a German who hadn't learned much English or Dutch. The boy was told to help the man assemble a harrow, what we called a *drag*. It was one of the simplest pieces of equipment on the farm. Its purpose was primarily to smooth the ground by breaking up clods. It consisted up of several units made of steel rods welded together in a checkerboard pattern about six feet square. Steel spikes about six inches long were welded to the lower side of each unit. The three or five units had to be connected in the proper order because they were not identical. Dad wrote, "Center section was A-shaped, other sections were diamond-shaped, so all the sections had to be right."

Considering the relative simplicity of a harrow, assembling it might not seem like much of a challenge—there were no moving parts. Dad was always quick to observe the way things fit together, so at seven he was surely pleased to be asked to assist in assembling anything. He remembered that it wasn't until years later he found out the hired man hadn't known how to put the harrow together but couldn't tell the boy he didn't understand. The boy was sent to make sure it was properly assembled. Dad's mechanical bent was obvious early.

Dad also mentioned that in 1923, when he was ten, he cultivated corn for the first time using a team of horses, and that he set up a new side delivery hay rake with many moving parts—much more complicated than the harrow. After putting it together he used the rake to turn over hay after a rainstorm. By the spring of 1927, at the age of fourteen, he began doing field work in earnest. He remembered discing four hundred acres and planting eighty acres of corn with a one-row lister (planter). He didn't mention how long it took to do those tasks.

My dad's childhood experiences with horse-drawn machinery in the 1920s became his model for what I was asked to do in the 1950s. Gone were the draft horses—everyone was using tractors by my time. But the expectation that kids could do anything remained solid. Since Dad was trusted at the age of seven to make sure a harrow was assembled properly and was put to work behind the horses soon thereafter, it was natural for him to assume that his own kids could do something similar. Never mind the switch to motorized farming that had happened in the meantime.

By the late 1950s, farmers in our area of South Dakota were beginning to realize their standby implements might not be the best for their summer fallow. The one-way had moved the precious topsoil out of the middle of their fields and deposited it toward the outer edges—it was, after all, a one-way! If they kept using it, eventually there would not be sufficient distribution of soil for their crops. Beside the disadvantage of soil displacement, the one-way always turned the soil over in a manner similar to the moldboard plow used for generations. Weeds that were killed and wheat stubble from the last harvest were buried. In our dry climate, that trash would remain underground more than one winter without decaying, and the bare ground above would be subject to wind and water erosion.

After my summer of mastering the one-way, Dad's innovation gave me a different job the following summer, using the Noble blade. Its simple design featured a V-shaped blade about ten feet wide attached to a heavy steel frame and balanced on two rubber tires. The blade was pulled through the field at a depth that could be as much as twelve inches, controlled by the tractor's hydraulic system. The advantage of the blade was that it would not turn the soil over, rather lift it a little leaving the dead weeds or wheat stubble on the surface. A single line in the dirt was left by the vertical bar holding the blade. The trash left on the ground helped protect the soil from erosion before eventually being composted to enrich the soil.

Dad bought the first Noble blade in Jones County, and in 1956, I was given the summer role of pulling it behind our U tractor. He had discovered this implement developed by Charles S. Noble, an Iowa-born farmer who had gone to Alberta, Canada, to farm. The village of Nobleford was named for him, since he was the largest landholder in the area. But in the depression and drought of the 1930s, he had lost 30,000 acres of farmland to foreclosure. He had recovered through his invention of the Noble Blade, a heavy piece of steel equipment that efficiently cultivated the soil.

Compared to pulling the one-way, the Noble blade was a little more difficult for me to judge exactly where to drive. There was no furrow to put the front tire of the tractor in—only the lifted soil from the last round. My older cousin, Melvin, was always quick to point out any lines of weeds he noticed I had missed by driving too wide. But during that summer when I was thirteen, I became as proficient at using the Noble blade as I had been using the one-way the year before.

Dad's Noble blade was a hit, and his relatives and neighbors soon got their own. But that wasn't all for Dad. Shortly after he got the blade, he found another slightly older Canadian invention, the rod weeder which was pioneered by John Deere. In 1929 George Morris in Saskatchewan had developed the much lighter piece of equipment which was first drawn by horses. It had a rotating rod about an inch square and ten or twelve feet long suspended on a steel frame with a steel wheel on each side. It was also submerged into the soil to kill weeds and loosen the soil.

In the heavy South Dakota gumbo, the Noble blade could do the initial work of loosening the soil in the spring after it had been packed down by the snow. Then the rod weeder could work it again in the summer when the soil was not so packed. The Noble blade and the rod weeder made a perfect pair. I am not sure whether Dad had the first rod weeder in Jones County, but he had an early one. He bought it from an implement dealer in Kadoka, the Jackson County seat a few miles west of our home.

Many farmers in the area began using the Noble blade and rod weeder in the years after Dad set the pace. At the time I didn't think of myself as being at the forefront of anything or being part of any experiment. I was just doing the work that needed to be done on our farm. But my opportunity to be one of the first people in our area to use the Noble blade was a part of a much larger revolution in dryland farming than I could have imagined. A *Wikipedia* article says the Noble blade was one of the most important agricultural inventions of the twentieth century, and that variations of it are still being manufactured by all farm equipment companies. The Noble blade and its counterparts have taken the place held by the moldboard plow for generations.

Although I had no idea we were at the front of a great change in dryland agriculture, I wasn't oblivious to other things in the world. I saw tourists swarming by on US 16 going east or west, and when my work was near the highway, I waved to the passers-by, wondering where they were from and where they were going.

Sitting for hours at the tractor steering wheel, I also had time to think of many things. I particularly remember considering how what I learned while working might relate to sermons I would eventually deliver. I can't say that anything I thought up at age thirteen was ever very useful, but I was especially fond of an idea I got while pulling the Noble blade. To look ahead helped me keep the rows straight and keep the rounds I was making uniform. In order to prevent missing strips of ground and leaving weeds standing, it was important to keep my eyes focused a bit into the distance instead of just looking down at the ground where I was, and then having to make abrupt corrections. Expanded to life, the idea of keeping a straight course is a true value—*keep your eyes on the goal.*

By the summer I was fourteen, I was well-accustomed to my role as tractor driver. That spring one field of winter wheat did not look good, so Dad worked the ground again and planted a spring crop—oats, I think. But ten acres of the wheat field looked good. Dad kept it and then promised it to me as payment for my summer's work. Although there wasn't much to do with it until harvest except look at it, I was pleased to know it would be mine. That year my field had the best yield of the season, about thirty bushels per acre. So, I was able to put a few hundred dollars in the bank.

Before the summer was over, our family's decision to move to Oregon was made—somewhat reluctantly for Dad, I am afraid. Before we moved in the fall, we were still preparing for and planting a winter wheat crop to be harvested the following summer. Before the wheat was all planted, I went ahead of the rest of the family to start high school in Oregon. Thanks to the sale of my wheat, I had enough money to buy some of my own school clothes, get my bike repaired, or do other things I might want to do.

I am grateful for the opportunities farm work gave me to grow and to learn. There were always emergencies to face or problems to solve while driving the tractor. If trash gathered around the bar of the Noble blade or the rod of the weeder, I had to stop, clean things off, and get going again. There was no one there to tell me what to do or to assist when it seemed difficult. I had to figure out the solutions as things came up.

Regardless of the family John Deere tradition, I became quite fond of my constant Minneapolis-Moline companion those three summers. The company was sold twice, and the Minneapolis-Moline brand name was dropped in 1974. I feel a little nostalgia whenever I see a picture of a rusted remnant of that family of tractors; it is a pleasant memory.

I am still pleased to report that I spent the whole summer I was twelve one-waying and lived to tell about it. When I was placed on a tractor in front of the one-way, I had no thought of how Dad's experiences had preceded or encouraged mine. Or when I sat down on the tractor seat in front of a Noble blade at thirteen, I had no idea I was a part of an agricultural revolution. I was just doing our work. Generation-to-generation farm experiences were important to me and to many others. Unfortunately, the opportunity to pass on those experiences directly terminates when the family is no longer on the farm, and I regret that I was unable to give those experiences to my own children, except through the stories I write.

Wearing a tee shirt my brother Gene found for me—to remember, in my old age, my youthful experience.

THIRTY-ONE

Celebrating Christmas

Our Okaton community was fairly homogeneous. We were all White until the mid-1950s when the Crazy Bear family moved in. We were all Christian, although not everyone was actively involved in a congregation. So, Christmas was a universally celebrated holiday. The churches in town were Catholic, Methodist, and Reformed, with a country Lutheran church on a hill several miles out of town. Our Reformed Church was the largest and strongest. People went their separate ways on Sundays but had no major conflicts with the public celebration of the winter holiday. We knew nothing of Hanukkah—I knew of only one Jew, who lived in Pierre. He operated a small clothing store. Islam and other world religions were unknown to us—far away and in places to which we sent missionaries. Kwanzaa had yet to be created.

There was always an evening Christmas program at the school. It included each student doing something—reciting a poem or other memorized piece, playing a part in a skit, or singing a song. Although religious Christmas carols were not forbidden, the school programs centered more on the secular accoutrements of the holiday: Santa Claus, Rudolph the Red-Nosed Reindeer, Frosty the Snowman, Jingle Bells, cookies, Christmas trees, and presents. Besides the program, there was a school-day party with a gift exchange. The students drew each other's names, but the givers and receivers were kept secret. Each child brought a gift for the one whose name he/she had drawn. Often Santa Claus arrived to pass out the gifts before we had our cocoa and cookies. I remember one year I recognized Santa's shoes, so I knew he was actually my teenaged uncle, Ted.

The school's celebrations were small compared to our church's Christmas Eve program. It was probably the community's biggest production of the year—a project of the Sunday School. The typical Sunday lessons were suspended for a month or two as we prepared for the program. Kids we hadn't seen on Sunday since the last Christmas season were suddenly there to take up their parts in the program. Their families were Dutch and considered to be part of the church, even though not attending regularly.

Various people in the church, especially the women, took the rotating responsibility for organizing the yearly event. The drama and content of each program depended on the imagination and creativity of that year's organizers. There were pieces to memorize for recitation, group songs to practice and learn, and invariably a reenactment of the manger scene with Mary, Joseph, shepherds, wise men, and angels. The baby Jesus might have been an actual little sister or brother, but more often he was a doll belonging to one of the girls—not so likely to disrupt the flow of the pageant as a real baby.

The conclusion, and for the children the most anticipated part of the event, was the distribution of bags of goodies to take home. Special Christmas candy was in each brown paper bag. Broken into bite-sized pieces were the hard rock candy, made in long cylinders with a consistent design in the middle, and the ribbon candy. There were always other candies, nuts, and an orange. Dad's brother, Uncle Bill, was recruited year after year to take responsibility for the candy bags. He was like those children who showed up only for the Christmas program. We never saw him in church during the year, but he was always ready to take his place on Christmas Eve.

A major part of each year's program was the pageant—different each year. The many programs blur in my memory, but details of two of them especially stand out in my mind. When I was in about fourth grade, I surely had a part—perhaps I was a shepherd or a wise man. But what I remember most is that my parents had the assignment of creating a lighted Christmas star to hang overhead. We had only recently gotten electricity in our home, although the church had been connected years earlier. Mom and Dad took their task seriously, puzzling over how to make an electric star. They worked on it at the kitchen table after we children were in bed. It is obvious which part each of them played in the design— Mom the artistic and Dad the technical. How to make a respectable, five-pointed star with no protractor and no high math? Mom worked at it until she got a design she was satisfied with—about seven and a half inches across. Each of its triangular points was a little thicker than the standard star everyone learns to make with five straight lines drawn by pencil.

Meanwhile Dad was working out how to light the star. Its shape would be cut into the bottom of a cookie box. (These cubical cardboard containers, about fifteen inches per side, had a top that closed neatly. They came to the stores filled with bulk cookies, so such boxes were always boxes available.) After Mom's design was carefully cut into the bottom of the box, a bare electric bulb was mounted inside, and the star's cutout design was covered with white tissue paper. Plugged in, it was indeed a credible star and one my parents were proud of. Years later Mom gave me a silver cardboard replica of her design with her handwritten note on the back, "Christmas Star we figured out in Okaton."

The other pageant that stands out in my memory was when I was in sixth or seventh grade. It was time for my cousin Alice Mae and me to be Mary and Joseph. Rev. Moget, the retired pastor from the Netherlands was serving as the only resident pastor in memory. One year while he was with us, instead of having an active, moving manger scene, the plan was for the children to be a motionless tableau while the pastor read a very extended version of the Christmas story from the King James Bible. I stood in the center of the scene while Alice sat beside me. The others stood or kneeled around us. I had been strictly instructed by my Aunt Grace, if I remember correctly, to stand perfectly still. I found that to be very difficult, but I complied by locking my knees and staring at the pastor as he read on and on.

Aunt Grace was in the front row, and she saw that I was not doing well—about to faint. There was no curtain to draw, but Grace got to me, led me off the platform and outdoors where the cold air soon revived me. I have no recollection of what happened to the rest of the tableau or how the long reading of scripture was concluded. But I doubt that program design was ever considered again. I know that I learned a lesson about not forcing myself to stand so rigidly, and to date, I have never fainted or even come close.

The celebration of Christmas in our home was always a high point of our year. The season had not yet become as commercialized as it is now, but the Montgomery Ward and Sears Roebuck Christmas catalogues did arrive before Thanksgiving. We children drooled over them; we wanted every toy. But we managed to pick some things to ask our parents for. Sometimes our wishes were granted, and sometimes not. One big gift I remember requesting for several years before Gene and I received it jointly was a toy farm set. It had a barn, a fence, and all sorts of animals. It was a much more perfect than the farm we lived on.

There were less expensive gifts—toys and gadgets—in the catalogue of Wisconsin-based Miles Kimball. There we could find gifts for our siblings. Never before Thanksgiving, but on that afternoon or the next day, we would draw names. Then each of us would pick out and order a gift for one of our siblings. One year I had Gene's name, and I ordered a bird whistle. It arrived in the Miles Kimball shipping box that Mom monitored carefully to keep each of us from learning what our own present might be. I was excited to be giving Gene this special item. But when it came time to wrap the presents, the whistle was nowhere to be found. It was so small that it must have been discarded with the packing material and was probably incinerated in the barrel halfway between the house and the barn that we called the burner. Mom gave me something else to give to Gene, but I always regretted the loss of what I had chosen for him.

We never had visitors on Christmas Day, and we had no tradition of a special meal for the day; we ate what we had. But on Christmas Eve we always had oyster soup made with much milk. Fresh oysters were available at a store in Murdo only during that season. A pre-Christmas family culinary tradition was making Gizzies, a roasted mix of nuts, pretzels, and Chex cereals. We also helped Mom make the Christmas sugar cookies using cookie cutters shaped as a star, a Santa Claus, or a circle. They were all topped with red and green sprinkles. We always ate well, although my sister hated the oysters and dreaded having to eat them as a meal.

Every year we decorated a real Christmas tree we had purchased in Murdo or Pierre. Before we had electricity, our trees had no lights. But they were always well-adorned—many colored glass balls, plastic icicles that glowed in the dark, cranberries on a string, little bells, and shapes we had cut from tops of tin cans. Aunt Bert, Mom's sister, annually sent us a box of holly, mistletoe, and evergreen branches from Oregon. We would have enough to dress our home and give some to the church.

Stockings were hung in the living room, and on Christmas morning, we children were allowed to retrieve whatever was in our stockings before our parents got up. We waited for everyone to gather around the tree to open wrapped presents. In later years we were allowed to open one gift on Christmas Eve before the program at the Church.

On Christmas afternoons we usually visited Grandpa and Grandma Roghair's home where we would see many uncles, aunts, and cousins. Our grandparents' family traditions had been established in the late 1920s and 1930s when life was particularly hard. Consequently, they did not have a Christmas tree. Presents in their home were deposited in a large cardboard box. They always remembered each of the grandchildren with a one-dollar bill in a Christmas card that was recycled from those they had received the previous year, but with the name of the sender cut off.

One Christmas, Grandpa was eating something special—I don't know whether it was a gift from someone, or whether he had ordered it for himself. But it was unbelievable to us; Grampa seemed to be enjoying Limburger Cheese. It was the strongest smelling cheese I had ever encountered. The cheese must have been a taste he had acquired from his own parents who had immigrated from the Netherlands. There is a Limburg in the Netherlands and in Belgium just across the border from each other. Needless to say, he didn't have to share that delicacy with the children.

It became an American tradition to wish for a White Christmas—especially after Bing Crosby's popular song of 1954. In my childhood, I remember many snowy Christmases. I even remember one year making the trip to Grandpa and Grandma's home riding in the back of the farm truck. I can't remember why we didn't use the four-wheel-drive Jeep. Another Christmas was distressing; there was no snow, and the wind was blowing hard. The farmers were worried that the soil in their fields would blow away. The winter wheat seeds had been planted in September, and the plants had already made their appearance above ground. Would the crop make it to spring without the snow cover?

We had snow every winter, but not always by Christmas. But one year we even had a heavy snow fall by Thanksgiving. Old friends of Mom and their children visited us, and we children fashioned an igloo in our back yard. We also went sledding and tobogganing down toward our frozen dam. We still had snow for Christmas that year.

My childhood memories of Christmas are a joy to relive. We never had a lot of money, but life itself was rich for us. I can't imagine happier memories than those of my Christmases past on our Okaton farm.

THIRTY-TWO

Gumbo is Tenacious Dirt

The word *gumbo* conjures up various things, but the gumbo that residents of Western South Dakota know is not a stew made with okra, nor a southern Louisiana patois of the French language. It is the soil on which we walk—a peculiar kind of dirt that may have to be experienced to be believed. And once experienced, it is not easily forgotten.

The gumbo I grew up with is fertile and dark gray. It can support the growth of a wide variety of crops as long as there is sufficient moisture. The climate is semi-arid, with a yearly average liquid precipitation of a little over twenty inches, including the forty-five inches of snowfall. In a normal year there is sufficient moisture for grains such as wheat, but not for corn or fruit trees.

Of course, growing up on the gumbo, we took it for granted. When we went out of the house during or after a rain shower or while snow was on the ground or melting, we always wore overshoes. These were eight- or ten-inch-high rubber boots that slipped over our shoes and fastened with steel buckles. The things were never fashion statements, and yet we all wore them. In bad weather, they cluttered the entryways at home, church, and school.

Gumbo is deceptive when wet. We were always amused to see how unprepared to deal with ordinary mud our visitors from other places could be. They would wear normal shoes when it rained, and then expect to scrape them off to enter a building. But gumbo is a dense clay devoid of sand and becomes especially sticky when wet. Walking in it could double the size of one's footprints. It clings to the bottoms and sides of shoes making feet feel heavy and clumsy. Walking in it, a small child can find the weight of the mud to be an immobilizing trap.

Gumbo continues to cling after it dries, and it can't be knocked off by banging shoes against a wall or post. Once dried, it has such a grip that it takes a knife to cut it off. We learned early the characteristics of our dirt and weren't usually caught by surprise. If it started to rain when we were away from home in the car, we knew we had limited time to get home without getting stuck.

One particular gumbo experience clings to my memory much as that dirt stuck to us. In the Spring of 1957, I had completed eighth grade, and was the only one to graduate from Okaton School that year. I was to be honored at the county graduation ceremony in Murdo in early May. But my parents had informed the county superintendent of schools that I would miss the event, because we would be on a trip to Oregon. I was disappointed, but I knew the trip was important. Other trips to the West Coast had always been in the fall after the winter wheat harvest and after the next year's crop was planted. This time we were going to *scout out* the territory and confer with Mom's Oregon relatives. The decision had been made that we were going to move in the fall, so we would complete this trip as soon as school was out and before we started our summer farm work.

We were packing and planned to leave in the early morning. When it started to rain the afternoon before, my parents made a quick decision that we should get our luggage and ourselves into the car and leave before the roads got too wet. We indeed left as quickly as we could. Our 1949

Ford Custom sedan, that had already made several trips to Oregon to visit Mom's family, was filled with the six of us and our luggage for a two-week, 3,000-mile round trip. Only a mile and a half of dirt road lay between our home and US Highway 16. But about a quarter mile from home the car became mired in the already-wet gumbo. As we tried to go forward the mud packed in above the wheel wells, and we were stuck.

Being fourteen and the oldest kid, I was dispatched to walk back through the mud to our house and get the four-wheel drive Jeep. With its deep wheel wells and high ground clearance it could usually make it through the mud. So, I came back and shuttled the rest of the family home.

After changing our clothes, Dad, Gene, age twelve, and I went to work to get the car out of the mud while Mom and the two younger children, Crysti, almost ten years old, and Wally, five, were left to wait and wonder. We tried pulling the car with the Jeep; we tried pulling it with the tractor; nothing worked. We jacked up the car, took off the wheels, dug the mud out of the wheel wells, and put the wheels back on. It was useless. We toiled until dark that day, all of the second day, and into the third day. Neighbors seeing our predicament came with their tractors and attempted to pull the car. The gumbo would not let us go. As the days went by, I secretly wondered if I might make it to my graduation after all; we could always drive the Jeep to Murdo. But I didn't say anything.

On the afternoon of the third day Mom, waiting at home with the little ones, was considering giving up on the trip in exasperation. Then the sun came out and shone brightly. Gumbo *is* mysterious; as suddenly as it had become impassable mud two days earlier, it began to dry. Dad recognized the opportunity, hooked the car behind the tractor with a log chain, got on, and told me to steer the car. Gene was in the passenger seat. Dad pulled the car over some hardened shale in the road ditch and up onto the sod of unbroken prairie. Within a few minutes he was in the car with Gene and successfully driving across the prairie. I followed with the Jeep. When we reached Highway 16, he sent me back to the house with the Jeep—we left the tractor to be moved at a later date. In the Jeep I brought the rest of the family to the highway. Then everyone had to wait in the car for what must have seemed a very long time while I returned the Jeep to our house and walked the mile across the prairie to the highway. Once I arrived, we were off. Our trip had finally begun!

Of course, the wheel wells and underside of the car were still plastered with drying mud, to say nothing of the body and windows. Dad stopped about thirty miles into our trip at a gas station in Kadoka to wash the car. There were no commercial car washes in those days, but Dad knew the station owner and made some arrangement for the use of water. He hosed off the mud as well as he could, and we headed west. As the remaining gumbo under the car dried, clods bounced on the road behind us. Often Dad, seeing the clods in the rearview mirror, called out to the rest of us to look back at the trail we were leaving. We spread Jones County dirt all the way to Oregon and all the way back.

We were familiar with the nature of our soil, but we did not expect it be quite so reluctant to let us go. Despite the gumbo's hold on us, we did move in the fall. It was to be a difficult transition for us all. I have often thought about the gumbo. I miss it, but I have never worn overshoes again, and I can't say that I have missed them very much.

THIRTY-THREE

The End of Childhood–A
Trip on the Hiawatha

I was excited to be embarking on an adventure in early September 1957; I was fourteen. My whole family–Dad, Mom, and three siblings–boarded the train with me to find my seat and say good-bye. We hugged. It was late at night, so I was kissing everyone's cheek, comfortably repeating a family bedtime ritual. But when I got to Dad, he gently pulled away. I felt his embarrassment. A not-too-distant memory flashed into my mind: I had grabbed Dad's hand when we were on the sidewalk in Murdo, but I felt his thumb disengage my fingers. Neither of these responses shocked me, but on the train, I suddenly became aware that my relationship as a child was ending. Dad's unspoken message was clear: we men don't kiss. I was no longer a boy. At five foot ten and 120 pounds, I was a gangly young man, perhaps more obvious to everyone else than to me.

To get to the train my family had driven about 175 miles north of our farm to Mobridge, South Dakota. By that time the Chicago, Milwaukee, St. Paul and Pacific Railroad (Milwaukee) depot there was our closest passenger connection. The town had been named in 1906 perhaps by accident. The railroad abbreviation, *Mobridge* that indicated the location,

Missouri River Bridge, became the town's name. In the station on the east side of the river, I was boarding the celebrated Hiawatha train westbound on its transcontinental route from Chicago to Seattle.

I could not remember riding a train before, although when I was a toddler, my mother had taken me to visit her parents in Salem, Oregon. On that 1944 trip the trains were full of soldiers going to and from their war assignments. Mom told me how they "made a fuss over me" as I walked up and down the aisle of the passenger car. But now I was traveling by myself to McMinnville, Oregon. I would arrive in time for my first day of high school in a community I barely knew. Our family plan had been finalized after the trip to Oregon in May. I would stay for two months with my mother's sister, Alberta Whitworth (Auntie Bert), together with her husband Harold, and his son David.

The rest of my family would come in about two months, after the sale of our household goods and farm equipment. They would pack up the remaining family belongings in the small farm truck. The new 1957 Ford car would pull a two-wheeled trailer loaded with a freezer full of meat and vegetables from our farm and garden. The freezer would have to be plugged in overnight at motels on the way. Since it would be a long drive, Uncle Harold took the train to South Dakota to join them, and he drove the truck for our family.

Our move was the culmination of much discussion and argument; as a family we were jumping off into the unknown. Many factors had contributed to the decision. Most of Mother's family had moved to the Willamette Valley of Oregon during World War II for better employment opportunities. They urged us to come. Mom was passionate that her children should receive good high school and college educations, and Oregon seemed to promise that. We had all been impressed by a concert in the Murdo Auditorium given by a male quartet called "The Four Flats." They represented George Fox College, a small Quaker school in Newberg,

Oregon, a few miles from McMinnville. Mom envisioned her children as students there, not realizing that there were numerous colleges in the area. (We all did go to college, but none to George Fox.)

Mom, like other farm wives, had felt the isolation of the farm—one neighbor woman had recently committed suicide. Besides these issues, Dad's farming had not been prosperous. He later reminisced that he should have worked harder to get more land to farm. But still, it was a hard decision for him, since he was uncertain how he would support his family in Oregon. His own father was a more successful farmer than Dad, and Grandpa adamantly demanded that we not leave. Nevertheless, in spite of the uncertainty and dissidence, I was on the train to become the first of our family to begin a new life in Oregon.

We had spent a few sleepless hours in hotel beds before going to the train station. It was after midnight when we said good-bye. I was both exhausted and excited. My family disembarked, before the train began to move, and I settled into my seat in the dimly lit coach. Soon we were speeding west into the night. Daylight arrived as we made our way across the southwest corner of North Dakota before the broad expanse of Montana.

Somewhere near Bowman, North Dakota, I began to feel sad, and perhaps I shed a tear. I was leaving behind all that I had grown up with. As a deeply loyal South Dakotan, I couldn't imagine living in any other state; it was the only home and community I had known. I was already missing the farm and my family, even though I knew they were to arrive in Oregon in about two months. I was excited about the adventure of this trip, but that was tempered by a fear that I would never see South Dakota again or have any place so dear to me.

My adolescent experiences of the last year had been rich. On our family's brief spring trip to Oregon to prepare for our move, Aunt Bert had introduced me to two of her neighbors, Kay and Sandee, who would start high school with me. Armed with these two acquaintances, I hoped to be ready to meet the rest of the class. The previous summer of 1956, both of Okaton's nearby towns had celebrated fiftieth anniversaries. My brother Gene and I were part of a square dance exhibition for Murdo's celebration. Later I played the Hawaiian guitar and sang "The Rock and Roll Waltz" with my three siblings at Draper's event.

In the summer just ending, I had traveled in the back of a farm truck to a three-day 4-H camp in the Black Hills. I met my first girlfriend, Judy. We played volleyball and walked the paths together. Other campers proclaimed that the next year Judy and I would be the camp queen and king—something to look forward to. But now I was on the train to Oregon. Would I ever even see Judy again?

Beside the youth activities, I had worked hard on the farm that summer, driving the tractor, and doing most of the summer fallow work as I had the two previous summers. The ten acres of wheat Dad had given me for my summer's work had brought me about $800, a lot of money for me. I had enough to buy some new school clothes and to purchase other things I might need. The rest was in a savings account. But the summer was over, and now I felt very much alone.

Holding onto what was familiar to me, for the day and a half train ride, I had chosen to wear the fanciest cowboy shirt I have ever owned. Light green and long-sleeved with a dark green yoke and cuffs, it did not have ordinary flat buttons with exposed threads but smooth dark green buttons with shanks on the back hiding the threads. Typical Western multicolored stitching decorated the yoke and collar. It was the real thing. It had been my dress shirt in eighth grade, not for church on Sundays, but for Saturday 4-H club meetings and for the countywide events a few times a year. I wore it when I learned round dances while meeting and dancing with girls from clubs across the county. For the train ride I felt comfortably well-dressed.

I wore the cowboy boots we had bought in a small shoe store in Pierre, South Dakota. My feet were so narrow that the proprietor had fitted me with boots from his stock of women's sizes, otherwise there was no other gender distinction. How I loved those boots. They were black with small red and white floral inlays near the top. I had worn them on the farm, and they were well-scuffed. But I always smeared a heavy coat of black paste polish on them and shined them up for 4-H events. They were on my feet for the street square dancing at the Murdo anniversary, too. Shirt and boots, I was ready for Oregon.

Even though our train was travelling a day through the cowboy country of Montana, the passengers on the Chicago to Seattle Hiawatha were not locals. Perhaps they saw me, dressed as I was, to be an authentic specimen of Western life, while I just felt well-dressed. People were friendly to me, noted my attire, and wanted to know where I was from and where I was going. There were no other youngsters traveling alone, so the travelers were curious. I enjoyed the attention and was not bashful to tell them my story.

There was much to explore on the train beyond my assigned seat near the middle of the fifteen or twenty-car passenger train. I could walk from car to car, listening to the clacking of the iron wheels on the steel rails, all the way back to the baggage car, or venture forward almost as far as the modern diesel electric locomotive pulling the long sleek train. I could sit in the Super Dome observation car and look out the upper windows to view the sky, day, or night. From my assigned seat below, as we traveled west, I saw the scenery of prairie and sage brush give way to mountains and forests.

In the elegant dining car, I ordered what I liked. I had only known two Negro brothers living in our county, one of whom had stayed in our home while he was doing some excavation for Dad. So it seemed unusual to me to see so many Black Pullman porters working on the train. They were all refined, friendly, and helpful men. The Hiawatha was the top of the line in 1957.

Dad, always an avid reader and informed on geography and technology, had encouraged me to watch for the change of locomotives in Harlowton, Montana. From there for the next 440 miles to Avery, Idaho, an electric locomotive powered by overhead wires pulled the train through the mountains before a diesel was employed again. Either because I found everything else so interesting, or because I was sleeping, I missed the change Dad had wanted me to note. Often, I was unable to observe details that were so interesting to him.

After travelling about halfway across the continent to Seattle on the luxurious Hiawatha, I transferred to a less elegant train for the rest of the trip to Portland. I bought a sandwich on this train, but neither the menu nor the dining service was as fine as on the Hiawatha. When I finally arrived in Portland, I was glad to see Aunt Bert and David waiting. They helped me load my luggage, including my bicycle, into their station wagon. We then drove the last 35 miles to McMinnville, to begin my new life in the town of 7,000.

Aunt Bert was wise enough to make sure that my cowboy shirt was not laundered. If it had been clean, I surely would have worn it for my first day of high school. But she understood what I was yet to find out, the ribbing I would get from the other kids. Unfortunately, she was not able to confiscate my cowboy boots, and I wore them the first day of school. I don't know how many kids asked me where my horse was. I never wore the boots to school again. That small West Coast town was no place for western clothing!

I left my South Dakota home and childhood behind, but the memories I carry are a part of who I am.

The Roghair family shortly after our move to Oregon. Back l. to r.: Gene, Crystal, James. Front: Ed (Dad), Margaret (Mom), Wallace.

PART F

Looking Back

PART 4

Looking back

THIRTY-FOUR

Quilts—Lost and Found

When my mother died in 2012, a special baby quilt was proudly displayed on the wall of her room in the nursing home. The hanging may not have seemed remarkable to a casual observer; it contained eight blocks of the once-popular Sunbonnet Sue pattern. But this particular quilt told a unique story.

After she married my father in 1941, Mom settled into life on the farm. It was not easy—without electricity, indoor plumbing, or telephone. Mom had grown up in a town, was trained as a teacher, and taught for one year. At the age of twenty-four, she began to learn the responsibilities and expectations of homemaking in her new role as a farmer's wife. She enjoyed much of what was expected and did it well. But she could not accomplish everything she set out to do.

Mom acquired—maybe someone gave her—the Sunbonnet Sue quilt pattern. Before my birth, a year and half after her marriage, Mom began to make a baby quilt that was intended for my bed. She completed eight nine-inch square blocks of Sunbonnet Sue with different coordinated fabric appliques for the bonnet and dress in each block. She embroidered details in black and brown thread. Although she had done much work, the quilt was far from complete. Undecorated blocks of fabric were to be sewn between the Sunbonnet blocks, a framing fabric was to be placed around the outer edge to complete the quilt top, and finally, a backing was to be added. But making the eight decorated blocks was as far as she had gotten—her busy life had interfered.

Quilt-making has a long American tradition. It was often a social activity that a group of women undertook. Working together they would accomplish the task of making something useful, beautiful, and valuable. They had a good time doing it. But Mom didn't have such a group to work with when she tackled making a quilt on her own. Her solo project faltered.

More than fourteen years after starting the project she had four children, and the family was moving to McMinnville, Oregon. In the move, there was limited space in the small farm truck, the new Ford car, and the two-wheeled trailer it towed. Most of the farm and household property had been sold, but Mom had tucked away the quilt project—maybe she would still get to it someday.

Even though the quilt was intended for me as a baby, I don't remember seeing the blocks during my childhood. I first saw them in 2002 when I was fifty-nine. My brother Gene and I were helping our parents vacate their fourth McMinnville home as they were moving into a senior apartment in Hillside Manor. There was much to dispose of, and we quickly sorted piles for the Goodwill Store, the Presbyterian Church rummage sale, a resale shop, members of the family, and the trash barrel. Thankfully, Gene knew how to be decisive about getting rid of things. With no hesitation he put the quilt blocks in the Goodwill pile, and with a pickup load of other stuff they were gone. After about sixty years, the quilt blocks were now only a memory.

But Mom had not forgotten, and while she and Dad were settling into their small apartment, she asked about the quilt pieces. Gene informed her they had gone to Goodwill. She was upset, but Gene answered, "Well, they're gone. There is nothing more we can do about that," and Mom had to accept that she would never see them again. If she breathed a sigh of relief because she was no longer responsible for completing the quilt, she didn't admit it.

A few months later, Mom received an unexpected call from a woman she knew in the Senior Sewing Room in McMinnville. The caller wanted Mom to come and verify who had made certain quilt blocks and where they were from.

The group had received some quilt pieces that had been made in the 1930s. They were apparently made for a *memory quilt*—something a group of friends would work on together and then give to one of their members who was moving away. Among these quilt blocks some had been carefully sewn or embroidered, but some were less decorated or merely signed in pen. Regardless the artistic quality of the individual blocks, they were all to have been sewn together—quilted—and given to the friend who was leaving. That quilt had never been completed until the circle in Oregon received the blocks.

After her visit, Mom wrote in a diary page, "I recognized each name and handwriting on the quilt blocks." They were her old school friends and relatives from Timber Lake, South Dakota. Apparently, these blocks had also been in Mom's possession and a part of the pile of things that included the Sunbonnet Sue quilt blocks taken to Goodwill.

But how had the senior quilters tracked Mom down? Mom continued in her diary, "Through a long process! Only one block bore the town of the person making it. This was a small town in Oklahoma, so they had contacted the churches there, and someone knew the maiden name of the embroiderer. It so happened that she and I went all through grade and high school together in the nineteen twenties and thirties and still keep in touch. So, she was able to give the Sewing Center my present name and telephone number."

The quilt block that had provided the clue had the name of Corinne H. Minton—whose married name had become Smith—and the town was Hunter, Oklahoma.

These blocks were surely made by the Timber Lake friends to honor Corinne who was about to relocate to Oklahoma. So her new town was the only one named on a block; the rest of the group were staying in South Dakota. Probably the friends intended to get together and finish the quilt. They would give it to her to take along or send it to her. But the 1930s were desperate times; maybe Corinne left Timber Lake in a hurry. Perhaps she was getting married or had the promise of a good job—a brief minor oil boom occurred around Hunter in the 1930s.

Others in the group went their own way, and Mom ended up carrying that unfinished quilt with her through the decades and across the country. Maybe she thought she would finish this quilt sometime—but she never got to it. She had little passion for quilting. In the Sewing Center, she was pleased to see the completed memory quilt, but didn't feel she could pay the asking price to buy it.

If seeing that quilt weren't enough of a surprise, when Mom looked around the Sewing Room, she discovered that her own Sunbonnet Sue blocks had also been acquired by the group and quilted by a member, Becky Sauder. There was the completed quilt Mom had intended for my baby bed. The work had been well done, and the quilt had already been promised to someone for seventy-five dollars. When Mom saw it, it was as if a long-lost family member had been found. Mom and Dad negotiated, and even though it had been promised to another for a higher price, they were allowed to purchase it for fifty dollars.

Thereafter, Sunbonnet Sue was hung in their apartment, and as my parents' care needs increased, the quilt moved with them. After Dad died in 2006, Mom spent about six years in a private room in a Coos Bay, Oregon, nursing home. She was always proud to have the little quilt on her wall. On the day she died, my nephew, Chris Shoji, and I carefully took it from the room along with the few other personal items. My sister Crysti Shoji kept it for several years in her Coos Bay home but then decided I should have custody of it.

This quilt has never covered a baby's bed, but the small note in Mother's handwriting pinned to it these many years is a reminder of its remarkable lost-and-found tale. It became my challenge to piece together this story. The resources I relied on include Mom's brief note pinned to the quilt, the diary page my sister found, and then some internet research on Ancestry.com, and articles on memory quilts and Sunbonnet Sue. At first, I was totally baffled by the scraps of information, but I believe I finally got the story right.

What does Sunbonnet Sue offer us in our uncertain times? Even in times of pandemic or other uncertainty, Sue might again be the inspiration that *Classic Sewing Magazine*, 2016, remembered her to be: "During the Great Depression Sue's popularity reportedly skyrocketed as people yearned for reminders of simpler times."

I hoped that someday a sleeping baby in our family might finally be covered by this Sunbonnet Sue quilt, and thus fulfill my mother's original dream for it. As I complete this manuscript, my son David and his wife Adrienne have had a foster child in their home for an extended time in Utqiaġvik, Alaska. I entrusted Sunbonnet Sue to them, and they hung her near where this foster child slept and where another child might sleep in the future. Perhaps they feel the quilt is too precious to put on a bed where it might be soiled. But after all these years, I think my mother would be proud the quilt is being used, however that is.

The lost and found Sunbonnet Sue quilt (37X54 inches),
begun by Mom in 1942 in South Dakota, and completed in
McMinnville, Oregon, by the Senior Sewing Circle in 2002.

THIRTY-FIVE

The Prairie is My Garden

My grandmother Crystal Bowder and her two oldest children, Frances and Alberta, are depicted in Harvey Dunn's most famous painting, "The Prairie is My Garden." My mother Margaret, the third child, told us that she isn't in the picture because, "I was little. I was playing down in the draw," the gully on the left side of the picture. Her words sound as if quoted from her father Frank explaining to his young daughter why she wasn't in the picture. Mom often repeated her connection to the picture; she was proud of it. What an honor to be part of this iconic work of art, considered by many to be South Dakota's unofficial state painting!

Our family has hung prints of Dunn's piece in our homes for many years. A large copy used to hang over the fireplace in my parents' home in McMinnville, Oregon. My sister Crystal has one in her living room in Coos Bay, Oregon. My son David had one in his log home in Tok, Alaska, for several years. I have one in our adobe style home in Santa Fe, New Mexico. It is a family tradition which my cousins on the Bowder side remember from their parents' homes, as well.

On a trip to South Dakota in 2000, my wife Elizabeth and I hoped to view Dunn's original in the South Dakota Art Museum on the Campus of the South Dakota State University in Brookings. Alas, when we were there, it was not available. Instead, we saw a large collection of Dunn's World War I military magazine covers. They were in quite a different style from his famous prairie pictures. To date, I have had to be satisfied only viewing prints of "The Prairie is My Garden."

A few years ago, I received a newsletter from the Yamhill County Historical Museum in McMinnville, Oregon, where both of my parents had volunteered much time before my father's death in 2006. I was amazed to see a small black and white print of Dunn's painting in a notice for "Quilters," a play coming to the Gallery Theater in McMinnville. Years earlier, my parents had both been volunteers with the community theater as well as with the museum. I wondered if anyone in either organization had heard my mother's story about her family's connection to Dunn's painting. Or did those Oregonians even remember my parents' relationship to both of their institutions? That experience prompted me to write this chapter.

The belief that this painting is a depiction of our family members is borne out by family memories. Mom remembered hearing that the artist had been painting in Dewey County, South Dakota, near Timber Lake where she grew up. She said Grandma remembered seeing a young man making sketches. Historical documentation corroborates that in the early 1920s, Dunn may have been in their community—about the time Grandma and her daughters were of the age depicted in the painting.

Besides the remembered historical evidence, Mom always said, "That is *just* the way our house was, and the little draw out front was *just* like that." For Mom, the painting also reminded her of an important family event: She was certain that the little prairie house in the right background of the picture was the one that had blown over in a severe 1926 Fourth-of-July wind when she was nine. It was the night before her first brother Clifford was born. Too bad Dunn wasn't around to record the overturned house.

Younger members of our family were convinced as well. My cousin

Charlotte Bowder Rose, who has lived her entire life in Oregon, and was the closest of the cousins to our grandma, shared her evidence. She wrote, "The woman . . . depicted in this painting was holding a large pair of shears. Grandmother told me that these were the shears she won as first place for her best baking powder biscuits—and we all know Grandma's baking powder biscuits. So I, for one, believe it's more than likely this was an accurate depiction of Grandma, Frances and Alberta—the house and landscape could have been anywhere but the woman with the scissors, I do believe that was Grandma. I do not know who got Grandma's shears, but I saw them. Grandma used them almost daily. I used them to cut paper dolls at the table, and Grandma used them to cut patterns for the endless clothes she was making, or quilt blocks she was cutting out."

It is great to have family stories to tell about Dunn's art. I always tell guests to our Santa Fe home of our family's relationship to the painting. New Mexico guests accept my story, but that may not be true if we were in South Dakota instead of hundreds of miles away.

My most recent purchase of a print of the painting was at the famous Wall Drug, the small-town store just off Interstate 90 that grew, by ingenious worldwide advertising, into one of South Dakota's biggest tourist destinations—after Mount Rushmore. At Wall Drug there is a mixture of quality merchandise and cheap souvenirs, entertainment from crude humorous mechanical animations and a restaurant that still offers a nostalgic five-cent cup of coffee. When I picked up the print in the store's art section, I mentioned our family's connection to "The Prairie is My Garden." The young saleswoman smiled and replied, "Oh yeah. Every family in South Dakota thinks that is a picture of their family." Did that clerk mean our story was not true?

Dunn did not identify any of his models. Most of his painting was actually done in New Jersey, after his yearly summer trips to South Dakota to observe and sketch. Recent historical research suggests that Dunn arrived at a farm a bit of a distance from Timber Lake, worked there for a time and then disappeared. Members of that family have been identified as the models for this picture. Could that be true? Or could it be that Dunn did not intend to paint any particular family? Was his painting really *any South Dakota woman?* So many South Dakotans have claimed her and her daughters as their family.

I am glad the early twentieth century prairie and its inhabitants continue to come to life for us through "The Prairie is My Garden." I am proud of the legendary belief of our family that my grandmother and my two aunts are there for everyone to see for years to come.

Perhaps somewhere, Harvey Dunn is happy that he has touched the lives of so many. Maybe the mystery of his subjects is just what he intended.

I display my print of "The Prairie is My Garden," by Harvey Dunn. According to family lore, the mother and children represented are my grandmother Crystal Bowder, my oldest aunts Frances Bowder Storm, and Alberta Bowder Whitworth—all now deceased—at their home near Timber Lake, Dewey County, South Dakota, in the early 1920s. Margaret Bowder Roghair (my late mother) said she was a little girl and hiding in the draw behind her mother and sisters.

THIRTY-SIX

Fun Writing the Obituary

On the morning Mom died in September 2012, she was still breathing when I arrived at her bedside. Crystal had alerted me that it was time for me to come. She and her family had been looking in on Mom daily for several years. Now she was taking a much needed, short but long-planned, out-of-state, vacation with her husband and another couple. I had taken early morning connecting flights from New Mexico to get to the nursing home near my sister's home in Coos Bay, Oregon.

When I arrived in her room, I spoke to Mom, but she did not respond. I sat down beside her bed and sang a verse of "Amazing Grace," recited the Twenty-third Psalm, said the Lord's Prayer, and sang a verse of "How Great Thou Art." She did not stir, but as I sat quietly for a few more minutes, I noticed that she had stopped breathing. Quietly, with no drama, she was gone. Perhaps she had been waiting for the permission to go that these familiar words and music, in my voice gave her.

I quickly called to share the news with my siblings, then family members of Mom's generation on both sides of our family. I also phoned a few of my older cousins asking them to share the information with their families and emailed most of my other cousins.

One of my calls was to my uncle Ted Roghair in Kentucky. He was

259

the second youngest of Dad's eleven siblings. Ted reminisced that my mother had been his first-grade teacher. It took me by surprise, because I remembered Mom's story of Dad's youngest brother, Bob, being in the first grade. Mom, the new teacher, had asked the pupils to draw pictures of their families, and Bob just kept drawing more and more people. When questioned, he explained the size of his family, and it became Mom's introduction to the family she would later join.

That story about Bob had been clear in my mind. But Ted had just told me that Mom was *his* first-grade teacher, and he had responded to my query, "No, I don't think Bob was in school at that time." I didn't question Ted any further and assumed I must have remembered Mom's anecdote incorrectly. After all, who could forget his first-grade teacher?

When Crystal got back from her short vacation, we worked together in her office on the obituary. Confidently, I wrote up a draft to be shared with my siblings and then delivered to two or three newspapers in Oregon and two small newspapers in South Dakota—the *Timber Lake Topic* in the town where Mom had grown up, and the *Murdo Coyote*, serving Okaton, where Mom had moved to teach the primary room and lived for fifteen years as a farm wife.

With Bob, several of my cousins, and their offspring still living in the Okaton area and likely to read the Murdo paper, it seemed particularly important to mention Mom's earliest connection with Dad's family. Straightforward as that seemed, sorting out the story became more complex than expected, and it provided some lighthearted diversion for my siblings and me.

Since they were not present, we emailed the draft to our brothers for their comments. We included Ted's information that Mom had been his first-grade teacher. Crystal had not focused much on Ted's assertion but had made a mental note of the discrepancy with her own memory of what Mom had always said.

Gene was the one to challenge us. He emailed, "I wonder if we should check with Bob. Mom always said it was Bob that went on drawing pictures of his family. Ted has always been a little *out there* in his thinking, and he may not have gotten better with age."

I quickly responded, "Gene, that's an interesting take. Would you like to call Bob? . . . They both graduated in 1950, and Bob skipped a grade—I think you might be onto something. If my math is right, Ted should have started in 1938 and Bob in 1939, which would have put them both in her class, Bob as second and Ted as third grade. Check my math. Let me know, there is likely time to correct it before the *Coyote* goes to press."

Gene wrote back almost immediately, "I just got off the phone with Bob. He says he was in the third grade with Mom, and he thinks Ted was also. Bob says his first three teachers were Bennett, Bonesteel and Bowder, so he knows it was the third grade for him." Within minutes Gene wrote further saying, "If you can't get it corrected for the *Coyote*, at least it would have pleased Mom. She always enjoyed pointing out all the errors in the *Coyote*."

After doing more calculation, I concluded, and later verified to my satisfaction, that neither Bob's assertion that he was in his third year of school nor Ted's that he was in the first grade during Mom's year of teaching was correct. I emailed Gene, "The math of what Bob says and the memory of Ted both seem faulty. . . So I think we ought to correct the *Coyote* before it goes to press by changing the sentence, and make it say, 'Margaret met Ed Roghair, the oldest brother of her two elementary students, Ted and Bob,' and let it be. We don't have to figure this all out, but we don't need Bob and Ted both getting after us about the details."

I had barely gotten this email off, when Gene, tongue firmly in cheek, wrote, "Maybe we need to get Bob and Ted on a conference call and get it worked out." Then still working on the order of the three teachers Bob remembered, Gene wrote, "Maybe it only took Bennett and Bonesteel half a year each to find a husband."

I countered, "Might very well be true, then one of them would have helped Bob do first grade in the fall and the other, second grade in the spring—geniuses, both! Well, I'm sticking with the noncommittal suggestion I made a little earlier! But I will let you get Bob and Ted on the conference call if you prefer. I'm staying out of it."

The conversation ended with Gene's backing down on his own suggestion to get our two aging uncles to argue about who had Mom as his teacher in which year. Gene wrote, "I think I am going to defer to you on this one."

So, who could forget his first-grade teacher? Apparently, both of our uncles, nearly octogenarians at the time, had fuzzy recollections of exactly who his first-grade teacher was. Perhaps even Mom had forgotten the details, and we, the next generation, were unwilling to engage in the process of trying to verify the history.

Who would have guessed that writing an obituary could be so entertaining?

THIRTY-SEVEN

An Experimental Farmer and Beyond

Dad didn't do much writing; Mom often wrote for him. She used a typewriter well, and her penmanship, grammar and spelling were excellent, whereas Dad's could be puzzling. I found something that was probably prompted by Mom, but in Dad's own handwriting—a rare autobiographical note he penned:

Why to Oregon?

> Why we came to Oregon? There were a number of reasons. There had been a number of poor years, pretty dry, with stripe mosaic in the wheat, so I was a little discouraged. The prices were not too good. Jim was ready for high school. The county kids were sort of wild with not much supervision. Peg's relatives were pressing us to come to Oregon. I could not get enough land. I had been too busy experimenting on raising better crops when I should have been getting more land. It just seemed the time to move.

Of course, there was more to the story. At Dad's 2006 memorial service, I expressed my opinion that within agriculture there might have been a better fit for him than farming. If he had had the opportunity for higher education, he might have had a successful career working with a state college as a part of the US Department of Agriculture Cooperative Extension Service. Listening to other farmers and learning from them, experimenting, reading, and passing on the newest discoveries on crops and farming methods—those were his passions.

After Dad was gone, I was surprised to come upon the paragraph quoted above that he had written a few years before. Would Dad have agreed with my opinion about what might have been? What he wrote seems to verify that he recognized that learning and experimentation were actually what interested him, and that was how he spent his time and energy on the farm.

It was 1957, and he was nearly forty-five when we moved to Oregon. The next few years were hard, as he tried to find his place in the new setting. He had begun to farm in 1927 at the age of fourteen after he finished eighth grade. Dad had become a local pacesetter. By the time I came along sixteen years later, the green and yellow John Deere farm tractors and equipment were like a trademark of our extended family. They would never have a red Farmall tractor or anything else made by International Harvester on any of their farms! As a child I thought of it as a long family tradition. Years later I found out that Dad had started the John Deere tradition which had then been adopted by his father and his five brothers who all became loyalists. They all then pushed back in the 1950s when Dad bought both a Minneapolis Moline and an Allis Chalmers tractor, teasing him for the yellow and the orange machines. Dad, the innovator, was undeterred.

Learning to farm in the dry climate of the western South Dakota prairie was a constant challenge. The choice of crops was a mystery for newcomers whose experiences might have been in much different climates. In 1925 Dad's family had moved from northwest Iowa's moist climate. They bought a small farm that had been homesteaded just nineteen years earlier as the first settlers arrived west of the Missouri River in the new state of South Dakota. His father, Henry, had unsuccessfully tried to grow corn in his first Dakota season. Only later did the local farmers discover winter wheat that had been bred in Siberia and the Ukraine and introduced into Kansas in the late 19th century by German Russian Mennonite farmers.

In the 1950s when I was in grade school our state-approved textbook noted that it was too cold to raise wheat in South Dakota. But even as we read that, all the farm kids knew that winter wheat was about all we were raising. Looking back, I wonder whether Dad was involved in the local acceptance of winter wheat as the best cash crop. It would have been his sort of project since he always read farm magazines thoroughly and kept up on new possibilities.

Learning to protect the shallow topsoil of the land was as important as a farmer's choice of crops—perhaps even more important. Although there was not much rainfall—almost none in the worst years—when it did rain it was usually a heavy downpour. Severe water erosion of unprotected soil could permanently destroy the natural value of the land. Farming practices that left the soil bare or that created downhill furrows of any kind would encourage soil to wash down the rolling hills.

Wind erosion was another issue, since there was an almost-constant northwest wind, often quite strong, and hardly ever any real calm. Soil that had been held in place by the native grasses for centuries or millennia, when exposed, became quickly airborne and delivered to another venue altogether. There are stories that a cloud of Great Plains dust passed over Washington, D.C. as Congress was deliberating soil conservation measures in the 1930s and likely had an effect on the legislative outcome.

Farmers' plows that had turned the soil over and left it open to wind and rain were one culprit. The practice of summer fallowing—keeping half the cropland unplanted in each season—added to the problem. Whatever implement was used to keep the ground tilled in the summer, even the Krause One-way Plow, left the fallow land susceptible to both wind and water erosion. Dad's acquisition of the Noble blade and the rod weeder that left wheat stubble and the dead weeds and grasses on the surface of the soil were the beginning of a solution to both wind and water erosion problems.

Dad was always a member of the Farmers Union a national organization that promoted farmers' cooperatives—both buying and selling. He was a state regional officer of the Farmers Union, served as a long-time board member of the Farmers Co-op Oil Company in Draper, and sold his grain through the Farmers Union Grain Terminal Association in Minneapolis, Minnesota. One summer he took our immediate family to a Farmers Union camp in the forest of the Black Hills where we all learned about cooperatives and had a good time with handicrafts, singing, and sightseeing.

With his innovations and leadership successes, it was hard for Dad to decide in 1957 that it was time to give up farming and move to Oregon. Mom had long felt a bit of an outsider in the Okaton community and isolated on the farm. She was concerned about her children's education, and the move to Oregon was to be a good opportunity for us children. With so many of Mom's family encouraging our move, making a change seemed the right thing for their marriage, and Dad consented, over his own father's strong objection. Yet for years to come, Dad continued to say he wanted to move back to South Dakota sometime, but that never happened.

Dad was sick the first winter in Oregon because of the switch from a semi-arid climate to the foggy, misty weather in McMinnville where it rained every day, all through the winter season. He didn't have a job arranged when we arrived, and he tried several things that didn't turn out very well. He worked briefly on a turkey farm. He was a salesman for a tool manufacturer and travelled in several states. He tried selling Farmers Union Insurance. He took a course to become a Maytag repairman but found that it was as lonesome a job as the Maytag ads said it was and not a good source of income. He even bought a pickup and tractor and plowed gardens in the town and occasionally removed snow.

Mom worked as secretary of the local Presbyterian Church for a time and then took a job for a few years in the library of Linfield College, located conveniently across the street from their home. With that connection, Mom became aware of an opportunity for Dad and encouraged him to apply to be the college's maintenance electrician. Dad had tried to get an electrician's license when we first moved to Oregon, but he was not accepted for the required apprenticeship because he was over forty years old. He was not, however, required to have such a license to do maintenance electrical work. The position was perfect for him. There wasn't a washing machine, dishwasher, or sound system on the campus that he couldn't fix. And he was always fascinated by the chance to talk to the students and the professors about anything or everything.

He stayed in that job and retired from the college after nearly twenty years. Dad was a man for whom no one was a stranger. He was always ready to talk with anyone, and his conversations were always interesting for the other person as well as himself. He had learned how to make things work at a young age and applied his ingenuity in useful and fulfilling work far beyond the farm.

THIRTY-EIGHT

Sharing the Love of the Land

As I began to write this memoir, about seven and a half decades into my life, I became more and more aware that the history of the Dakota homeland did not really begin in the early twentieth century with the arrival homesteaders on the new railroads, or with building of towns along the tracks. The history of the land extended back through generations of Native American tribes who had lived on the land for millennia.

In 1868, about seventy-five years before my birth, the Treaty of Fort Laramie was signed by chiefs of Lakota, Dakota, and Nakota tribes and representatives of the United States government. The treaty provided that all land west of the Missouri River, in what we now know as South Dakota, was given to the Cheyene Lakota tribe as a reservation. In that treaty, the United States government guaranteed protection to the tribes. Of course, when gold was discovered in the Black Hills in 1874 the treaty was quickly abrogated. Protection ceased. Railroads were built and miners and settlers swarmed over and onto the land.

A little over twenty years after the treaty, the Wounded Knee Massacre took place. As I was growing up, I learned about the battle, but to me it seemed to be distant and ancient history. There was only a sterilized version of the story to read in schoolbooks. But I now know that Wounded Knee wasn't distant from my experience. The battlefield is only a little over 100 miles from where I grew up. And the event occurred within a year of the birth of each of my four grandparents. No one in our school, community, or family ever discussed how the land we lived on became ours, even though Native American tribes had lived there for many generations before we arrived.

My place in the historical timeline seems ironic—my birth year was about halfway between the date of the signing of Treaty of Fort Laramie and the time I began to write this memoir. It has given me pause to recognize that the land I loved growing up had also been the beloved home of generations of Native American children and their ancestors long before the railroad came through bringing hordes of new people to use the land and its resources.

Like others, I have been slow to come to grips with the fact that the injustice done to the residents of Dakota territory was common to history throughout the United States. Native Americans almost always resisted the usurpation of their homelands, and many died in battles with the United States military, in individual skirmishes, or suffered the destruction of their villages being burned. Those who survived were crowded onto reservations, no longer able to use most if any of their ancestral land. They were expected to give up their culture and beliefs—to disappear into the White world. But they are strong people and, not surprisingly, they have not disappeared, although many White Americans today seem surprised to learn the indigenous people have not gone extinct.

Writing my memoirs, I cannot reverse history. I can only humbly acknowledge the history into which I was born. I can do my best to honor the proud history of Native peoples throughout the Americas and to thank them for their faithful stewardship of the land. But at the same time, I can also claim to share my own love of the land and to promote brotherhood and sisterhood with Native American neighbors. The South

Dakota prairies will always be my cherished childhood homeland, even though I recognize that long before my time—and yet not that long ago— those prairies were the beloved home of many Native American children as they were growing up.

When I was a child, I didn't question our presence on the land. The air we breathed was perfumed with the scent of "Manifest Destiny," the right, even God-given responsibility, of White people to take the whole continent and colonize it. This concept arose from application of the "Doctrine of Discovery," first promulgated by a fifteenth century pope. He declared Europeans' right to claim by "discovery" any land in the world not occupied by Christians. I now recognize that my opportunity to live in and to love the prairies arose from the actions of the United States based on that doctrine. But I also believe that it is not possible to square that doctrine with a theology or philosophy of justice, or with an understanding of universal God-given human rights.

So I dedicate the stories of this memoir not only to my own family, our community, and the land I grew up on, but also to past, present, and future generations of Native American children. They have cherished and will continue to legitimately cherish the land as their own home on the range. May we all share the wonder of this spacious homeland.

Appendix

THIRTY-NINE

Remembering a Homesteader

I wrote the following essay in the spring of 1957 as a part of the Jones County requirements for graduation; I was finishing eighth grade that year. With only minor editing, I transcribed this in 2018 from my handwritten work which was preserved by my mother Margaret Roghair. I remember sitting in the Lobdell home to interview Don. The house he and his wife shared was the last one on the Okaton townsite eastbound out of town on the original US Highway 16 or on the Milwaukee Railroad it closely paralleled. I believe it was the same house my parents had occupied briefly before the house on their farm was ready for occupancy.

Don Lobdell (1884-1968) seemed to enjoy the opportunity to tell his story to me. He was five or six years older than my four grandparents who were born between 1889 and 1891. He was born in White Lake, Dakota Territory; North and South Dakota were not admitted to the Union until 1889. Although there may have been other original homesteaders still living in the Okaton community when I was a child, he is the only one I remember to have had that history. I wish there were more such stories of the original homesteaders. I appreciate my mother's recommending that I interview Don Lobdell, and I am glad that she preserved my fourteen-year-old telling of his story that I can share.

Memoirs of Don Lobdell—by James E Roghair, 14 years old in 1957

In 1905 Mr. Don Lobdell came west in a covered wagon from eastern South Dakota. He homesteaded north-east of Draper and north-west of Vivian. In that same year he worked on the railroad grade from Chamberlain to Presho. He used a two-horse slip on the approach to the Chamberlain Bridge. When he got to Presho he graduated to a wheel-scraper. The lots were sold in Okaton and most of the other towns around in 1906, and the railroad was completed to Rapid City.

In 1905 he lived in a tent until he had built his 10x12 shanty. He was considered a "big shot" because most people only had 8x10 shanties.

His first post office was Moore, which was located about two miles east of the present town of Vivian. The mail was carried in a stage which was actually only a wagon or buggy pulled by a team. The supplies were carried on big "lumber wagons." Mr. Lobdell said he remembered them with water barrels on the side. They followed one of two trails, the stage trail which followed the White River, or the ridge road, which followed the ridge near where the railroad is at present.

Mr. Lobdell says one of the early winters was so bad he never saw a soul for about thirty days. The first winter he spent only $15.00. It cost about $15.00–$20.00 to build his shanty also. Three-year-old steers cost about $30.00–$35.00, and calves sold for $10.00.

He did a lot of freighting for homesteaders. He would haul their supplies to their shanties, many of which he had himself built. Often, he was called to Chamberlain to witness for proof that someone had lived on their homestead for the required length of time.

The year 1905 was very wet and crops grew exceptionally well. Mr. Lobdell said that gave many people a mistaken idea about how things grew out here.

In 1906 or 1907 he brought thirty-five or forty head of cattle across the river for his herd.

Once when he had been across the Missouri River his horse's leg was sprained. At Chamberlain it was so bad he could no longer ride. So, he led the limping horse as far as two miles east of Presho in one day.

The cattle got the "Texas itch" in one of those early years. The itch made them lose their hair. The only way to get rid of the itch was to dip them twice in a hot chemical. The dipping did the job, and it was lost.

Alkali was another disease among the cattle, horses, and hogs. They lost their hair, manes, hooves, and tails. The chickens got it too, and they lost their feathers.

Many homesteaders just proved up and then left. Some big ranches illegally paid homesteaders to prove up and then sell out to them.

In 1914 Mr. Lobdell moved to the White River bottom south of Okaton. There he raised alfalfa seed and ran some cattle.

He built his first threshing machine, which was simply a log with 2x2 boards nailed on it and in a wooden frame. It was turned by a kerosene engine. He used this machine on spelts and barley. After it went through this, it was cleaned with a fanning mill. The first person to use a boughten threshing machine for him was Mr. Fred Sears. Then Mr. Lobdell purchased a machine and became one of the main threshers in these parts. He threshed up until 1936.

On the river he had Mr. C. T. Bates, the Hughes brothers and Charley Smith for neighbors.

Mr. Lobdell said he was never lonely. The pioneers were all very fine neighbors. They made their own recreation. Once he rode a saddled steer for about a mile. After all the "buck was out of the steer" he got off from a "pretty tired steer." Mr. Lobdell said homesteading was mostly a lot of fun.

FORTY

Brother Gene's Story

I am glad to include this story by my brother Gene for several reasons. It is a good story that provides yet another look at how we lived when we were children. It verifies the truism that each person remembers the experiences and events of life differently. The circumstances of which he has written are only touched on by a sentence or two in my foregoing Chapter 6 "Chic Sale." I thank Gene for kindly giving me permission to publish this dramatic piece. Here is what Gene remembers:

McIntire—by Gene H. Roghair

At the top of the stairs, a baseball bat in my hands, I stood looking down the narrow stairwell toward the open door. From my vantage point, the lower half of the front screen door was visible at the foot of the stairs across the narrow hall.

I had just seen a man with a heavily bandaged head come up the driveway behind the wheel of an old Buick. If he came to the door I would be able to see the lower half of his body. His face had already excited my worst suspicions.

This was no normal summer day. The whole western part of South Dakota was in a nervous state of high alert. When Mom said she was going to take a nap downstairs, I had assumed this defensive position, without mentioning anything to her.

A stranger could approach the house by foot or horseback, from the east, south or west, but I had never known one to do that. The nearest neighbors to the south were several miles away, to the east a couple of miles and to the west more than half a mile. The only people who ever came from those directions were other kids on horseback or people coming in from our fields. With this in mind, I had stationed myself with my head hanging over the edge of my sister's bed. From there I could keep watch out the north facing-window, down the rutted driveway lined with stunted Russian olive trees. I would be able to see anyone approaching our driveway from the east or west on the dirt road that followed the section line. Ordinarily, no car came in either direction on that road unless they were on the way to our house.

At high alert, I had begun by reclining awkwardly on the bed in the silent house. Suddenly, confirming my worst fears, a totally unknown car had turned into the driveway. This would have been remarkable enough on a normal day. I pretty much knew by sight every vehicle in our third of the county. I also knew the cars driven by the Watkins man and the Farmer's Union man. Unknown cars usually belonged to traveling salesmen.

When the car turned in, I had immediately gotten to my feet and stood behind the curtains looking down the drive. From there I knew I wouldn't be noticed by the occupant of the car as it approached.

The automobile had moved much more slowly than one driven by someone familiar with the place. This tentative advance had given me time to evaluate the car and the situation. The time was the early 1950s, but the car was an old one from before the war. In addition to being old fashioned, it looked rough. Who else could it be but McIntire.

As the car passed the red fuel tank and curved left to approach the front door, I had clearly seen the driver. Middle-aged or older, he wore a huge white bandage wound around his head. It covered his hair, his forehead and most of his right ear. In a few seconds he would be at the, front door. It was already too late to run down the stairs and warn Mom. After days of nervous apprehension, it was all playing out in real time.

About a week earlier, a man named McIntire had escaped from custody in the Pennington County Jail in Rapid City, South Dakota. He had been arrested and was being held for the State of Kansas. He had initially been incarcerated on charges of strong armed robbery and rape. He now had the additional charge of jail escape. Believed to be armed, dangerous, and desperate, he was thought to have headed east into the treeless, and sparsely settled parts of western South Dakota.

Rapid City, with radio station KOTA, was one hundred and forty miles to the west, and, except for KGFX at Pierre, seventy-five miles to the northeast, it was our nearest radio station. Without telephones or other means of communication, inhabitants of the scattered farms and ranches stayed tuned to one or the other of these stations, hoping for updates. For several days, there had been no trace of the escapee in this or any other direction.

The situation was tense and put everyone on edge, but, for some time, there was no consensus about what needed to be done. It was summer in the middle of a busy farming season. Although men wanted to protect their wives and children, they couldn't very well stay home from work indefinitely. The men, alone on their tractors, also seemed vulnerable. The wives at home were worried about their husbands as well as themselves and their children.

People were not in the habit of taking the keys out of any vehicle. Cars, trucks, jeeps, and tractors were always left with the key in the ignition. Houses were never locked when the inhabitants went out. There were no deadbolts or other locks on the inside to protect the occupants.

At the Post Office, at the Church, at the grain elevator, over tractor wheels, through pickup windows, at Ladies' Aid and Women's Home

Extension Club meetings, men and women opined on the best plan of action. Initially, there was some talk of removing the keys. Most people soon dismissed this idea. It was thought that families would be safer if a desperate man were allowed easy access to an escape vehicle. Women and children would be safer if he were just allowed to move on.

There were various opinions about locking or nailing doors shut from the inside. It seemed wise to slow his access, but there were other considerations. Perhaps it was a minority opinion, but some thought hospitality was the best protection. Before his escape, McIntire was being held for armed robbery. That didn't necessarily mean that he was out to randomly slay anyone. The escapee was, no doubt, afraid and concerned for his own safety. If the desperate man had easy access to food, water, and transportation, it seemed probable that he would take what he needed and be on his way. Better to give him what he wanted and let him go. Why force him to choose between violence and seeking out the next farm or ranch?

I don't remember people talking about guns as a means of protection, but, when the old Buick with its bandage-headed driver went out of sight in front of the house, I had considered my options, and what my response needed to be. The only rifle in the house, a single shot .22, was hung on nails over the door to Mom and Dad's bedroom. Where the cartridges were, I had no idea. There was no use trying to get to the rifle, the stranger would be at the door before I had a chance. The shotgun, a single shot 20 gauge, was somewhere on the back porch. So the guns were inaccessible, and anyway, an armed confrontation seemed dangerous at best.

If the jail escapee didn't immediately attack my mother, my best approach seemed to be to stay out of sight until circumstances warranted my participation. At the age of ten or eleven, I was at a severe disadvantage, but I didn't really see it that way. I always thought of myself as pretty much grown up. If he went after her, my only chance was to strike unexpectedly from behind. My best weapon was the baseball bat I was holding. Some of the older girls at school were more effective hitters than I was, but I was confident I could swing it hard and straight enough to cause damage to a man's head.

By now, Mom must have been roused from her nap, and would be looking out the window to see who had driven up. Little Wally, the only other person at home, would still be napping in the tiny back bedroom.

Actually, Mom had gotten to the door before the stranger had a chance to knock. I could hear her snap the hook on the screen door that kept it from blowing open and banging in the wind. "Hello," said Mom.

"I'm looking for Mike and John Leitheiser," said the stranger.

I couldn't believe it. I was so ready for this injured stranger to be the criminal that, at first, I thought it had to be him anyway. But why would he want Mike and John? The brothers lived on a dilapidated farm about three miles to the north northeast. What would he want with them? How had he ended up at our farm? I couldn't imagine. But his bandaged head and disreputable old car didn't seem so out of place once I knew who he was looking for.

Mom said, "Half a mile east. Two and a half miles north, on the east side of the road.

"Thank you, ma'am," he said, and drove away.

After that, I became more relaxed about the escaped criminal. As far as I was concerned, it seemed like he had already done his worst. A few days later, the whole affair got resolved.

A kid about my age was riding in the back of a pickup and spotted a man in a very unusual place. He was clinging to the underside of a railroad trestle, up near the ties. A little further down the road, the kid stopped his dad by banging on the roof of the truck. When he reported what he had seen, the father went to the sheriff's office. The sheriff got reinforcements, and together they arrested the man and brought him in.

I was never quite clear where the trestle was. I always imagined it up towards Philip on the Chicago and North Western Railroad tracks in

Haakon County. I think I placed it there because I remembered riding under one in the back of a neighbor's pickup on the way to a Philip cattle auction. I imagined myself going under a trestle and seeing what that kid had seen. I wished it had been me.

A Footnote to Gene's story

As I was preparing the manuscript for this book, I received a message from Clarice Roghair, the wife of my oldest cousin, the late Melvin Roghair; she had been a part of our family for about fifty-five years. When she heard I was including Gene's story in my memoir, she wrote, "And the criminal McIntire, if we are talking about the same guy, I saw him walking down the railroad track past our place. My brother Stan was one of the two guys who found his hiding spot leading to his arrest. He pretty much followed the Chicago and North Western Railroad, if I remember correctly. But I do recall Mel [Clarice's late husband] telling about he and his brothers taking the keys out of the cars so the guy couldn't steal them. Jack [their father, my uncle] told them if the guy wanted the car, let him take it as long as he left the family alone. So, they put the keys back." Clarice then located and forwarded AP wire stories about the arrest and the part her fifteen-year-old brother, Stanley Caldwell of Wendt, South Dakota had played.

This was a huge event in our part of the world, but the fact that the family of my cousin's wife was involved in the capture was news to us. Gene and I were just kids at the time, and so was Clarice. This piece of shared history is a reminder that it is indeed a small world—especially in western South Dakota.

FORTY-ONE

Mom's Tale

I clearly remember the incident Mom describes in the following story from the late 1940s or early 1950s, and the surprise follow-up report a few days later. I believe it was after my sister Crystal's birth in 1947, and that she must have been the youngest member of the chokecherry-picking party described in this story.

Chokecherries are quite small, so there is little to show for the work of picking them. But the jelly from them is indeed wonderful when it is finally made. Mom's story was published in The South Dakota Magazine, July-August 2010 shortly before she died. Mom had done much writing but didn't get many articles published. I appreciate the opportunity to share this one.

The Last Chokecherry Picking—by Margaret Roghair

While making peanut butter and jelly sandwiches for our picnic lunch, I heard the happy voices of my two little boys through the open kitchen window. It was almost autumn and the tall prairie grass surrounding our Jones County farm near Okaton was turning brown—the time of year that rattlesnakes might be lurking nearby.

Family responsibilities hung heavy on me because my husband was busy in the fields, and he also served on various boards. The country was at war, so we were unable to get materials for a telephone line, and there was no easy communication in case of an emergency. I had single-handedly beaten out a grass fire that threatened to become a prairie fire when wind suddenly whipped burning paper from the trash barrel. And I saved one child from drowning in the watering tank, and another that had waded too far into the reservoir. But, we were able to buy a car—and today the kids and I were going to pick chokecherries with a friend—Fran, and her two little girls. As we traveled to Fran's house up and down the roller-coaster hills (we called the road passage "Tipperary" after the famous bucking horse), the meadowlarks greeted us with songs. Goldenrods nodded as if to say, "All is well this happy day." We watched an old eagle rise lazily from his lookout on a high corner fence post and soar into the blue sky. A snake slithered across the road, reminding me that danger was always near. If someone got bit by a rattlesnake, could I slash the skin with a razor blade and suck out blood before starting the 70 miles to a doctor?

Our car rattled over the planks of the old wooden bridge and Fran's big shaggy dog, hearing us approaching, announced our arrival. Fran tucked her two small girls into her car and led me across the prairie toward the corner of the school section where she knew chokecherries abounded.

We followed as her car bounced over crisscrossed car tracks on the prairie. We came upon a prairie dog town and watched the little creatures pop out of their mounds and stand on hind legs to peer at us. They would bark and scold, then scurry down their holes.

A few miles further and we had reached an isolated and sheltered draw, devoid of vegetation except for wild chokecherry that bordered the bank of a dry creek on the further side.

The children scrambled from the cars, eager to pick the tiny berries. Soon their faces were smeared with the purple juice and their lips puckered from the astringent taste of the wild fruit, and they were off to play. I had spread a blanket on the ground in the sheltered cove, and Fran and I took turns calling the youngsters back from the tall grass that surrounded this sheltered little spot. Here was a small world all our own with only our little ones and the songs of birds and the chirping of crickets to keep us company.

Then the solitude was broken by the sound of an airplane overhead. We recognized it as that of a rancher who lived farther on up the creek. He was making a routine trip to town. The children shouted and waved their straw hats and sunbonnets as the pilot tipped the plane's wings in response.

After we had filled our pails with the cherries and had our picnic lunch, we gathered our little ones and returned to our homes. I prepared the chokecherry juice and made a beautiful, clear jelly. The day was such a success, I considered writing a message on the jar's labels about our fun outing.

As I was contemplating, my husband arrived from town with the mail. He spread the "Weekly" in front of me and pointed to the headline: "Rattlesnake Den Discovered." I read on, "When Mr. Lynn Lyman was flying home to his ranch yesterday afternoon, he saw a gleaming patch beneath him as he flew over the dry creek bed in the corner of the school section where wild chokecherries grow. Closer scrutiny revealed a glistening, moving mass. To his astonishment he saw it was a mass of rattlesnakes. Instead of continuing to his ranch, he returned to town and summoned the state rattlesnake eradicator, and together they killed the snakes, numbering eighty in all. Rattlesnakes come from afar and gather into a den to hibernate in the fall, and it was not previously known that this thicket was their winter rendezvous."

We saved the jelly for special occasions, for we did not venture out again to pick chokecherries.

Editorial Comments

Why Mom referenced the country being at war is not clear; World War II had been over for several years. The Korean War did begin in 1950, but it did not affect day to day life the way WW II did. I believe we did have our party line phone by that time, but it wasn't a reliable way to reach help in an emergency.

My cousin Henry Roghair has lived his whole adult life on the same farm where I grew up, a few miles from Okaton. When he read this story, he declared it couldn't be true, because the swarming of the rattlesnakes and the ripening of the chokecherries would not happen simultaneously. I remember the snakes were indeed a surprise to our family, but the coincidence certainly did happen. The Murdo Coyote news Mom quotes is verification of the facts, and when I spoke of this story to one of Fran's daughters more than sixty years later, she remembered the chokecherry picking and the snakes, as well.

FORTY-TWO

A Family Tribute

It is my privilege to share my sister Crystal's poem. It is dated about two years before our dad died, shortly before his ninety-fourth birthday. She expresses her love and respect for our father from her point of view as a three-year-old. This poem is a tribute to her, to our dad, and to his whole family. The last surviving member of Dad's generation of thirteen siblings was our uncle Bob Roghair who died at the age of eighty-five in 2018.

My Father and the Promise—by Crystal Roghair Shoji

> A tall lean sunburned man
> Strides long on the prairie.
> Thick wavy hair
> Shining black as a crow.
>
> Soft brown eyes settle deep
> from prominent cheekbones,
> the hue of fresh turned sod.
>
> Khaki shirt and pants,
> And a toddler riding high
> In crook of his arm.

In nineteen fifty,
South Dakota is young,
a hopeful country.

The man has dreams for
beautiful wheat
and strong children.

In spring, the sprouting wheat
was new green in dark loam.
Birdsong filled the silence.

Now, a sea of stalks
and pregnant golden heads
rustle and sway with the wind.

The child burrows her face
into the rough twill
smelling sweat and tractor grease.

The radiant sun
Warms her head and back.
She crinkles her eyes
against its brilliance.

"Put out your tongue,
I'll give you a Sen-Sen."
He hands her one,
then a few grains of wheat.

The child puckers at
the soapy taste of Sen-Sen.
The nutty wheat
gums up as she chews.

The playful wind
catches her hair,
billows under the khaki.

She laughs in response,
raring her head back
to face the soft blue
and cotton sky.

Her eyes span the sky
where she studies the clouds,
looking for the elusive Jesus.

The man works his fingers
in the loose soil,
runs his hands through wheat,
then rests his palm
on the child's skull.

At this the child is still.
She senses that perhaps
if she doesn't move
the hand will stay on her head.

The man is gentle
with the wheat and the child,
rejoicing in the day.

Later when dinner is set,
he bows his head,
praying long with the cadence
of his ancestors.

Hands are held all around
while boiled potatoes steam up
and cool on the platter.

The man's words carry the child
away from the prairie
where countries wage war,
and hungry people need bread.

Now the child peeks
from under half closed lids
as he blesses
the wheat and the children.

The child understands
that she and the wheat,
the sun and soil,
are the prairie's promise.

Because she knows this,
she will be stronger.

I wrote this with my dad, Ed Roghair, in mind, but I think "the man" could easily represent any of the Roghair brothers who were my uncles, the sons of Henry and Cornelia. —Crystal Shoji, January 2004.

Printed in the United States
by Baker & Taylor Publisher Services